Curiosities of the Cityscape

Curiosities of the Cityscape

A Wanderer's Anthology

K. C. E. HARRISON

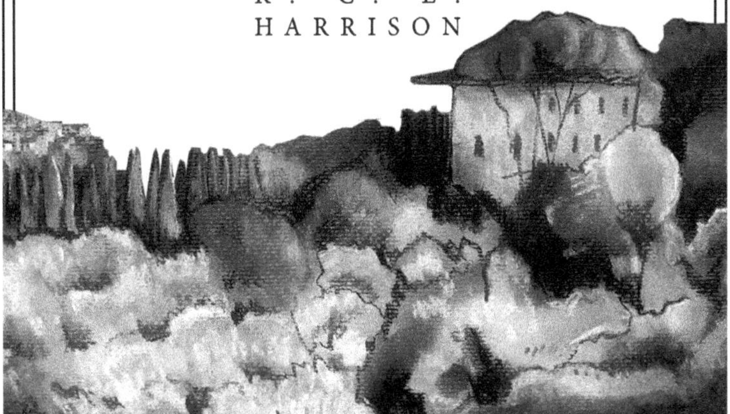

Published by K. C. E. Harrison Publishing

Book Cover by K.C.E Harrison

Illustrations by K.C.E Harrison

1st edition 2024

To my childhood self,

whose eyes beheld the world with wonder and whose heart resonated with curiosity,

and to my future self,

a guardian of my flame for exploration.

In dedicating this novella, I bridge the realms of innocence and experience, uniting the seeker of yesteryears with the sage of tomorrows.

The relationship between how we act and the spaces we're in shapes society. Life precedes space; it's our actions that give meaning to our environment. Understanding space entails recognising the primacy of human agency in its creation.

K. C. E. Harrison

Contents

Preface	XIII
Introduction	XV
Reflection in Observation	1
Day and Night and Dawn and Dusk	3
The Paradox of Sharing: Desires and Loss in the Cityscape	8
Tales from the Inverted Cityscape	11
Anchors in a Shifting Landscape	14
Unorthodox Windows of the City	16
Conduits of the City	19
Subtle Summons of the City	21
Engravings of Memory Architects	27
Picnic between a Traveller and Crow	29
Night's Illusion, Day's Revelation	32
Skies of Stone and Memory	35
Barter of Observations	37
When Time Takes Shelter	40
City and Contours of Transition	42
Internal Landscape of Silent Musings	44

A Tower's Night Tale 47

Keystones of Light 49

Passage Through the Crowded Throng 50

In the Embrace of Conversations 52

City's Balcony 54

A Lovers' Olive Odyssey 56

Shifting Perspectives by Wandering Left 58

Laughter of Languages 60

Shelved Perspectives from the Escarpment 62

Glimpses Through Gates 64

Exchanges of Transient Tokens 66

City Plumage 68

Lighthouses in the Night 70

A Pilgrimage to the Serpent and Crab 72

Straying Beyond City Limits 75

A Summer Day's Tale in the City 78

Candles and Oddities: the Charms of Solitude 80

A Reread 82

Supper for One in the Rose Garden 89

Moments of Centralisation and Abandonment, and Places in Between 91

Three Arches, Three Tales 93

FOTOAUTOMATICA 97

The Heron of the City's Waterways 99

Hills and Structures in Harmonious Play 101

Elegance in Stillness 103

From Riffle to Skyline 104

Patrol Beneath the Bridge 105

Evening Sonata 107

Sunday Streets 110

Performances of Poses and Preening
by Peculiar Pigeons 112

Notes of Kinship: An Evening Unfolds at the Café 114

Tales of the River and City 116

A Culinary Interlude 118

A Melodic Journey Along the River 120

Whispers in Brass 122

To be a River 124

The Conversational Arch 126

Arcade 127

Hitchhiker 128

A Day of Unexpected Bookstore Encounters 129

Thoughts on Cafés, Bookstores and Libraries 132
Echoes of Cityscapes 135
Interplay of City and River 138
Coiling of Streets 139
Interlude: The Rhythms of Departure 141
Gems Along the Bridge 143
A Reflection on Identity in Unfamiliar Lands 145
A Poem for an Evening 148
Tales of Urban Performers 150
Embracing the Winter Shift 152
Trilogy of Arches 154
An Encounter with a Dragon 160
Treasures in Teaspoons 164
The Crow's Call 168
A Recovery of the Lost 174
Reflections on Familiarity in the Cityscape 178
A Parting of Paths 180
Echoes of City and Kin 184
Acknowledgements 188

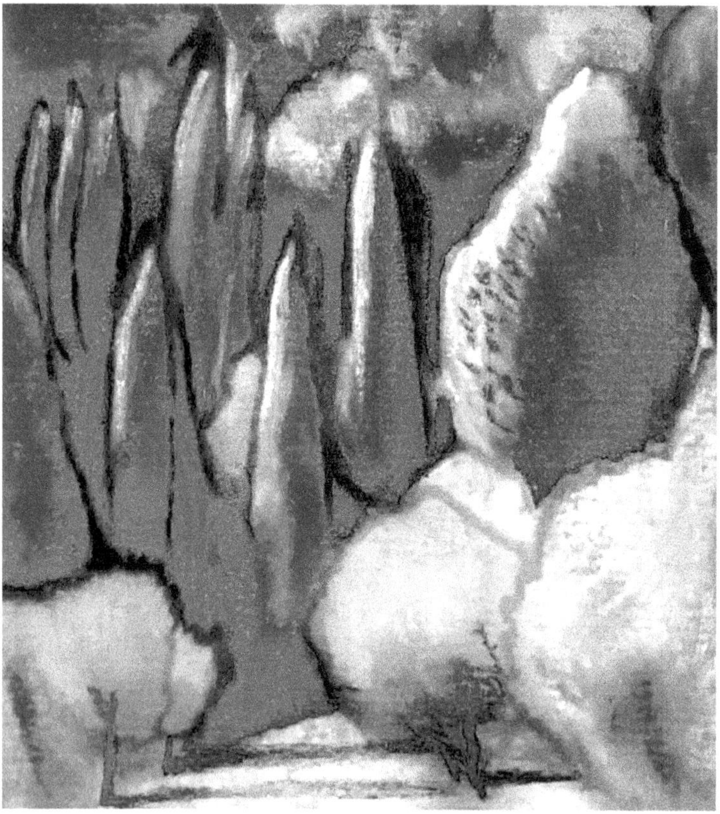

Presented to Irene. A reflection of your
vibrant spirit.

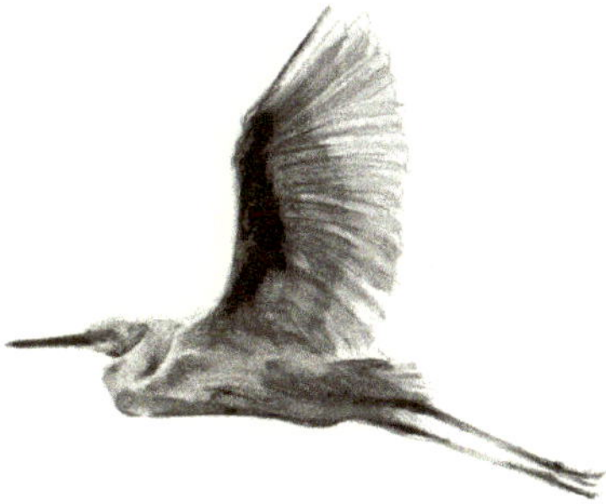

Preface

In the entanglement of memory and imagination, where stories take shape and dreams intertwine, this collection of tales emerges from where I first sat at Orti del Parnaso after wandering through Giardino dell'Orticoltura, Florence. As a graduate of the University of Dundee, holding a Master of Architecture with Urban Planning, my journey through the realms of design and urban landscapes has become a wellspring of inspiration for the narratives within these pages.

The inception of this book was born out of a passion for both the written word and the art of shaping physical spaces. Drawing on the nuanced interplay between the two, each story reflects a synthesis of my academic background and a deep appreciation for the visual arts. These narratives, while fictional, echo the resonance of the places I've studied, the designs I've envisioned, and the cities that have left an indelible mark on my creative spirit.

As a fervent advocate for the arts, I have always believed in the power of storytelling to transcend boundaries, offering readers a passport to worlds beyond their own. The chapters within this book are evidence to that belief, where the ordinary and the extraordinary coalesce to create an assortment of emotions, atmospheres, and characters.

While this work is a departure from the rigours of architectural academia, it encapsulates the essence of storytelling as a means to explore the complexities of the human experience. As you delve into these pages, I invite you to join me on a journey where the lines between reality and imagination blur, and the landscapes of both the mind and the cityscape intertwine.

To those whose stories have inspired mine, and to the readers embarking on this adventure, I extend my heartfelt gratitude. May these tales resonate with you as much as they have with me.

K.C.E Harrison

Introduction

For those with a penchant for inquiry, those who savour the subtle cadence of exploration, this compilation extends an invitation to traverse realms—an odyssey that goes beyond the confines of reality and fantasy. Here, the commonplace metamorphoses into the extraordinary, and the extraordinary ephemeralizes into a transient companion in the ravelled layers of life's adventure.

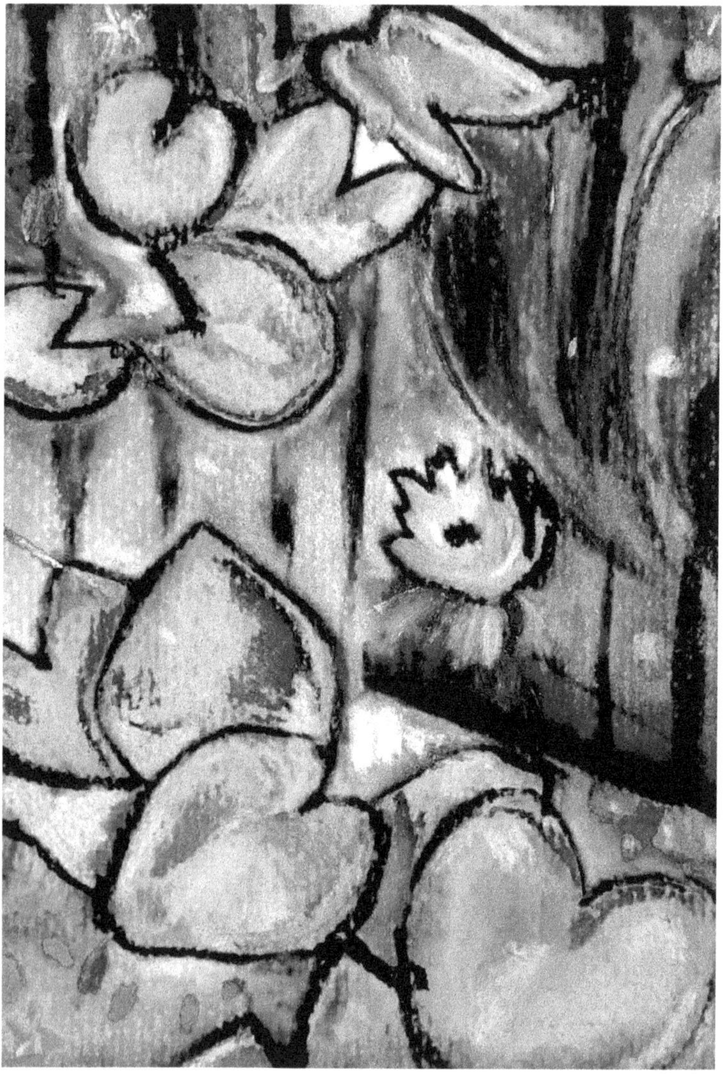

Reflection in Observation

Within the domain of human interaction lies the profound practice of observation, an essential tool for self-awareness and understanding. As the traveller navigates the intricacies of solitude, they embark on a journey of introspection, recognising reflections of their own essence in the actions of others. Observation serves as a window into the complexities of the human experience, offering valuable insights into individual and collective behaviour.

Through observation, one uncovers hidden facets of their identity, both known and unknown, as they encounter shadows of themselves in the actions of strangers. Through silent observation, individuals forge connections with unseen souls, finding a sense of unity in the shared experience of witnessing. However, it's essential to acknowledge that observation has limitations. The subjective nature of perception and the potential for bias may distort interpretations of observed behaviours, leading to incomplete or inaccurate understandings.

Despite these limitations, observation remains a valuable tool for self-reflection and understanding. By addressing biases, the traveller can navigate human behaviour more effectively, fostering empathy and connection in interactions. The impact of observation extends beyond introspection, influencing future interactions and choices. By immersing oneself in the crucible of human behaviour, individuals gain a deeper understanding of empathy and the nuanced dynamics of the human condition. Thus, observation emerges as a cornerstone of self-reflection and societal understanding, shaping individual perspectives and collective consciousness alike.

Day and Night and Dawn and Dusk

One cannot speak about Day without the discussion of Night. One cannot speak about Dusk without the discussion of Dawn. One cannot speak about the change from Day to Night without the discussion of Dusk and one cannot speak about the change from Night to Day without the discussion of Dawn.

There exists a puzzle of perpetual beauty — a puzzle of Dawn, Day, Dusk, and Night. Whilst each remains distinct, it is a tale told not in isolation but in a ritualistic order with no discernible end. Each of these partners allows for a nuanced portrayal of the city's temporal landscape. Its procession of light and shadow has no finality, no conclusive note to detect.

Let us begin with Dawn. One cannot speak about

the change from Night to Day without the discussion of Dawn. As the city slumbers, Dawn heralds a new beginning. The first light pierces the darkness, revealing the outlines of structures and streets. Dawn sings like songbirds, the promise of a fresh start, an awakening that whispers hope and anticipation.

A faction of Dawn springs as a visionary, a city planner, or perhaps even a master organiser. They embody the essence of Dawn as a time of preparation and birth, constantly working to bring order and structure to the city as it awakens from its slumber. Like the unfolding of a market square at dawn, this individual is the curator, ensuring that everything is in place for the day ahead. They facilitate Night's transition to Day, working tirelessly to create the base for a lively environment and fresh opportunities.

Conversely, Day is energetic, pulsating with life and movement. It is where the city paints its liveliest strokes. Where the hum of activity surrounds you as sellers perform sales of their wares. A faction of Day stands with a purpose through these markets, a physique of broad shoulders carrying crates back and forth stand out against the backdrop of shoppers hunched over stall items. They are ready to greet each customer with a warm smile and a sense of possibility. They are the passionate gardener tending to flower beds, breathing life into neglected spaces. Day is the time for renewal, for growth, a progressive force in the landscape.

As Day handovers to Night, we encounter Dusk. It's considered the quiet moment when the city catches its breath. Dusk is a liminal space: here, the skies of Day spill into the encroaching shadows of Night. Dusk is more than a simple transition; it acts as a bridge between two distinct periods while embodying them both. By exploring its various facets—the interplay of light and darkness, the shifting soundscape, and the subtle transformations—we gain a deeper understanding of this elusive time.

A faction of Dusk presents itself as the caretaker of transition. They are the planners who ensure safety as darkness cloaks the city. These manifestations can appear subtly throughout the city; a twilight keeper who sweeps away the debris of the day, the detritus of human existence that litters pathways. The gradual presence of street onlookers as they begin to arrive home. They oversee rituals and ceremonies that mark the end of Day and the beginning of Night— the vendors who engage in the delicate choreography of dismantling their temporary shops with practised ease. The journeys home, the dot-to-dot of lampposts who's light activates against Night. They are the storytellers, sharing tales of the day's events as people gather around the fading light.

Yet, one cannot speak of Day without the discussion of Night. Artificial lights cast a different spell on familiar surroundings. They are alluring beacons in the absence of light. The city reveals Night's unseen and ephemeral aspects hidden in plain sight. Sound appears more direct as it echoes on silences of streets. A faction of Night emerges as a figure who wanders the evening hours to bask in the relief of darkness. They are the artist, the poet, the dreamer who thrives when the world is cloaked in shadows. With each step, they bring liberation, a release from the constraints of Day. They are the solitary thinker, the insomniac philosopher who ponders the mysteries of the universe under the blankets of stars. Night is the time for introspection, for creativity, for delving into the depths of the soul to discover what lies beneath. This is where secrets secrete from indulgent sips, vulnerabilities and desires unfurl from Day's grip. It can be an uninhibited exploration of the self and surroundings when accompanying a faction of Night.

In this puzzle of Day and Night and Dawn and Dusk, each is an interconnected piece, relying on its counterpart for a complete narrative. The city's story is not merely a linear progression but a cyclical, complementary nature of temporal phases in place.

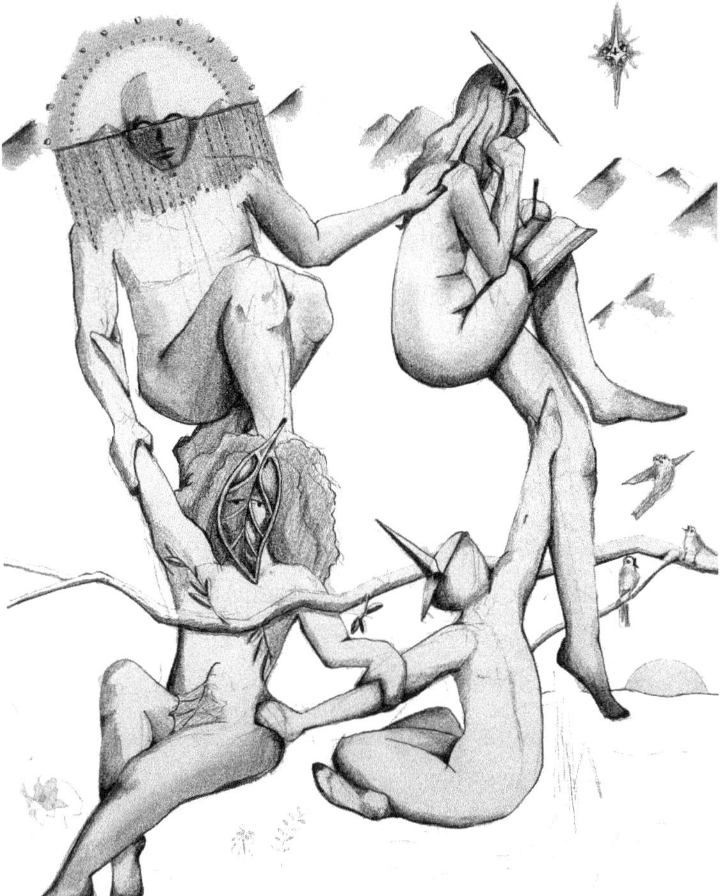

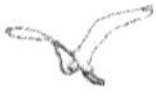

The Paradox of Sharing: Desires and Loss in the Cityscape

As feet touched new soil, the traveller to the city found themself entranced in continuous moments of pulsing life unfolding all around them. Where they passed, individuals were crafting memories—laughter shared in hidden corners, whispered conversations against the backdrop of city lights, and stolen glances that spoke of flittering sparks.

As the curious observer, a peculiar feeling crept its way in. It wasn't resentment towards the joy of others; rather, it was a longing for the exclusive ownership of moments that had previously existed only in the lands of imagination.

This envy bore a unique weight, for the traveller was navigating the city alone. The desire for treasured moments intensified as a sense of solitude lingered. In the familiarity of home, such moments might be shared with those who understood the nuances of one's past. Yet, now on unfamiliar streets, surrounded by groups of strangers creating their own mirage of experience, the traveller yearned for a collection of moments that were uniquely theirs.

The traveller coveted something for themself, something that no one else would take away from a travel like this. To find such a thing remained unassured but they would search for it. Would it present itself in the form of a physical item, a small, antique, brass casting perhaps at a flea market? Would it be an interaction with another traveller or a local? Something they could treasure, in memory or in hand. A pleasure from the taste of a home cooked meal, or a unique dish from a dimly candle lit restaurant perhaps?

Yet this desire to treasure a memory was entwined with a sense of loss when it was shared - a paradoxical cohesion that spoke the intricacies of the human experience. The traveller arrived at a nuanced understanding: while sharing a memory may compromise its individuality, it also imbues it with new layers of meaning and significance. Through the act of storytelling, memories surpass their singular origins and become part of a larger collective experience, augmenting both the storyteller and the listener.

These would all unfold in boxes of happenings the traveller would come to unwrap. This journey would not see them alone, but uncovering parts of the city and themself that were truly hidden in spaces the curious observer had not predicted.

Tales from the Inverted Cityscape

In the midst of the downpour that swiftly unleashed itself from the skies, the traveller debated whether to forsake the comforting embrace of their abode for an early-day escapade. Opting to wait until the rain subsided, they eventually braved the outdoors when the air still held a warm, ethereal glow, gently wafting through the city streets and cradling the ground below. Car lights casted blurred beams dimmed by this aquatic veil and the air rendered the buildings lining the streets momentarily monochromatic.

Eventually the traveller was given the pause of the downpour to begin their day. They opted for an unfamiliar alleyway, hoping to expand their mental map of the city. Along this cobbled way the traveller encountered puddles that glistened with an unusual luminosity. The traveller crouched to observe the liquid's surface. It reflected an almost molten-metallic silver, appearing denser than water. They felt a pitter of rain begin again, yet when the raindrops met the surface of the puddles they didn't join, they landed as drops would on a window.

Looking over to where drains met between pavements and cobbles, the raindrops trickled down into the below, but this unknown liquid seemed to be emerging from it. An uncanny phenomenon was unfolding—not a mere flooding of drains, but an orchestrated convergence of the substance toward the unsuspecting traveller.

What began as curiosity quickly transformed into a subtle panic as the encroaching substance moved with deliberate intent. The traveller nimbly hopped over the spreading liquid and navigated the uneven cobbled streets. It seemed to be joining, leaving little of the stone floor available for the traveller to step pass. The traveller hastened their pace, the end of the alleyway still a distant crossing. Buildings merged into one another, compelling the traveller to duck beneath the low arch of the tunnel they were sprinting towards. In the climactic moments of their dash, an unfortunate twist of the ankle left the traveller teetering on the edge of tumbling into one of these unnatural puddles. The traveller, seeing their shock in the liquid's reflection, mirrored the apprehension of facing the unknown.

As their visage drew closer to the liquid's surface,

silently bracing for an imminent plunge, the traveller felt an imperceptible force at play. A clandestine energy enveloped them, steering them away from the impending fall. A mysterious figure, seemingly materialising from the shadows, had intervened. Hauling the travelling up to two feet, their head and world spun.

However, language proved to be a barrier, as the figure's words were unintelligible to the traveller, whose immediate focus remained on expressing gratitude for averting the potential catastrophe, but turned back to the puddles that had now drained with confusion.

In their gratitude, the traveller failed to notice the transformative shift in their surroundings. Unbeknownst to them, while expressing thanks to the enigmatic saviour who emerged from the shadows, the city had undergone a peculiar inversion. The unfamiliar tongue of the man concealed a welcoming invitation, ushering the traveller into a realm beyond the mirror—a world where cities swapped places, and an uncharted adventure awaited their discovery.

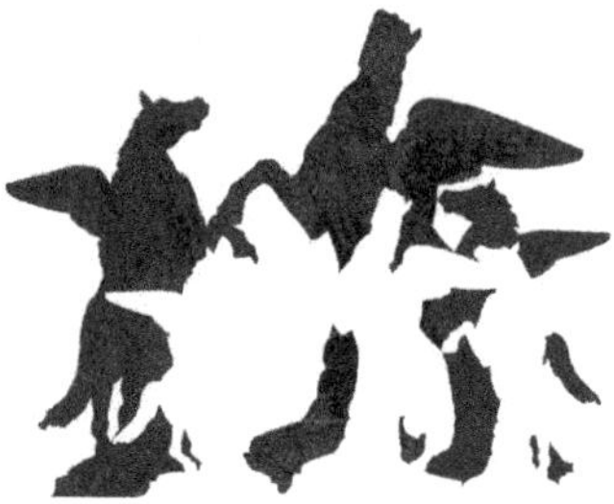

Anchors in a Shifting Landscape

Immortalised statues of stone or bronze found throughout the city cast long shadows upon every corner and avenue. Within a mere hundred steps, the traveller could stumble upon a frozen moment, an acknowledgement of history or a whisper of artistry. The traveller, in their hurried pace, might have passed by these without a second thought, or they may have paused, conscious of the statue's presence, and wonder its importance of standing there.

Names may stand alongside them, etched in plaques, but the reasons for their existence often remain enigmatic. They came in various forms – groups frozen mid-motion, animals captured in eternal grace, men and women gazing out over the city they've come to symbolise.

The traveller pondered. Perhaps, in the quiet depths of the night, they awaken, sharing stories or thoughts through an invisible, telepathic connection. Or perhaps, they remain perpetual observers, watching the city's performances unfold throughout the day.

Those found within the confines of buildings, meant for the eyes of spectators, were destined to be looked at but never walked past unknowingly in a happening. However, those positioned on the teeming streets, with their eyes in view of the passing throngs, were onlookers to a diverse array of human dramas. Did they grow weary of the routine, the endless cycle of day-to-day life? It's a question left for contemplation.

Amidst their grey and white hues, these statues had become anchors in a changing landscape. Some were adorned, dressed up for special occasions, while others were left to crumble, weathered by time and the elements.

A bronze boar sat at the hustling market, its nose lightened by the pets and scratches from those wishing for good luck on him. Pigeons often chose heroic figures who stood poised for landing points, perching on their outstretched arms as if these stone figures had summoned their companionship. In this simple act, perhaps, the pigeons conveyed a silent greeting, acknowledging the echoes of life that these statues represented.

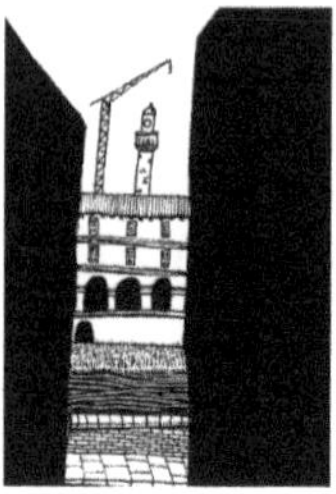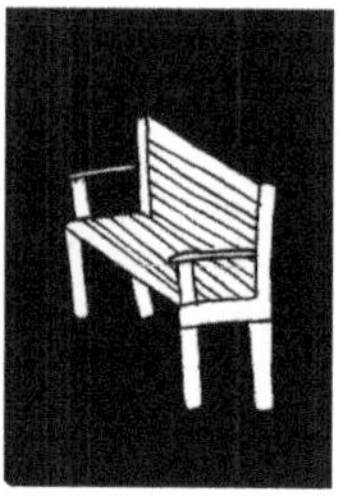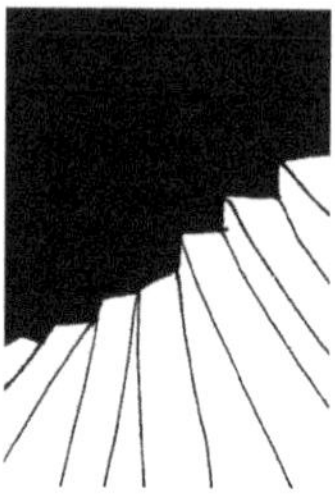

Unorthodox Windows of the City

Amidst the ceaseless clockwork of the city, the traveller found themself happening upon a series of pauses throughout their day. Each one akin to a window of a city's moment. Seated upon a weathered bench, originally sought for mere rest, the traveller discerned a subtle transformation as the bench itself assumed the role of a figurative window. This moment of respite and reflection revealed itself as an aperture for observation and contemplation for the traveller and their surroundings.

Devoid of glass or frame, it proved a unique vantage point, picturing the surrounding scene for a fleeting instant of repose. A pocket-park on one of the city's central streets, tucked behind layers of road that expanded just north of its centre. Yet, beyond this solitary example, various manifestations of these metaphorical windows scattered throughout the area.

Leaning against the moss-covered stones of a riverside wall or perched atop a flight of weathered steps, the traveller found themself afforded perspectives spanning the cardinal directions of the sprawling cityscape. However, it was upon ascending to higher elevations that a truly panoramic vista revealed itself.

From this elevated perch, the traveller's gaze extended across the meandering course of the river, the surrounding edifices serving as a natural frame for their contemplation. Their eyes traced sun-yellowed riverbanks, from the solid embankments to the graceful arches of a distant gallery, and upwards to the rooftops that boasted a clocktower and industrial crane skyward. For the traveller it prompted a contemplative journey from the terrestrial to the celestial, mirroring the traveller's own desire to retrace their path from whence they came.

On other occasions, the traveller found comfort upon the steps of a hilltop, the view illustrating the topography and collective nature of the cityscape built upon its natural landscape.

Each offered a distinct lens through which to perceive the cityscape. From the expansive vistas observed atop elevated staircases, to the intimate glimpses afforded in the midst of the crowded marketplace, where the frame constricted to only scents and flickers of merchants and merchandise. Movements of others distinguished the

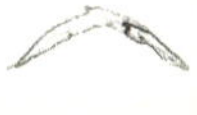

frames as they passed by the traveller.

A series of halts, manifested through physical structures or ephemeral moments of contemplation, offered the traveller opportunities to perceive and engage with the city. Whether they chose to was their own decision, as the halts were offerings, interludes for moments of reprieve and reflection.

Conduits of the City

The streets in this city were not only thoroughfares but intricate labyrinths of life. They could be narrow, barely wide enough for two people to pass by each other without brushing shoulders. They were flanked by tall buildings that seemed to reach for the sky. These towering structures created a sense of confinement, emphasising the closeness and crowding that ensued when the streets filled with people. At the time the streets were busiest they became funnels, directing the babble of humanity toward the centre of the city and its lively squares.

But these streets, despite their charm and history, posed their own unique challenges. The buildings, standing tall and grand, often had their windows protruding out onto the streets. Iron bars and metal gates protected these architectural extensions, casting patterns of shadows

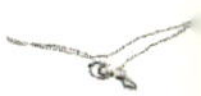

on the pavement. These metal guards, though essential for safety, only added to the complexity of navigating these crowded streets. Always a need to be aware of surroundings, whether the need to duck under the grates, or being aware of the change of levels from pavement to road.

As the traveller made their way through these charming but chaotic alleyways, they often felt as if they were wading through a slow, gunky liquid desperate for air with the slow strides from the pedestrians in front. There were opportunities for refuge on the street edge, in the spaces following structures protruding outward, there one could catch breath. The pulse and recede of people, a constant tide, dictated the rhythm of the city. When the traveller finally emerged into one of the squares, it was as though they had joined a flock of sheep being herded into a pen. It took a few moments to adjust the eyes as a ceiling of blue sky and sunlight blanketed the square.

In these moments, the traveller couldn't help but marvel at the paradoxical nature of the city – its narrow, confining streets giving way to these expansive and lively squares, offering both an intimate and grand experience of urban life. Each encounter, each winding street, added layers to their city exploration, and the traveller embraced it all, understanding that it was in these crowded streets and squares that the heart of the city truly beat.

Subtle Summons of the City

This city was peculiar in ways untold. The traveller noticed the intricacies of each brass fixture they passed. Some formed of mythical creatures with snarling heads, warning them against knocking. Others consisted of floral motifs with twisting brass leaves having once been alive before its petrification round the handles. The lion was a particular favourite; the little dopey lion, timid holding the new ring it swore to protect and the fierce beast mid snarl they knew too well would drop the ring the instant they reached for the knocker to snatch a bite. These were some of the many variations.

The scary faces seemed to ward off unwanted visitors, but for those who understood how to navigate the city's secrets, they were welcomed. In mythology, tales abound of dogs like Cerberus guarding underworlds, instilling a

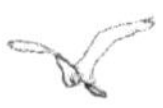

sense of protection amidst the tourist filled streets. Perhaps there was a similar significance to these fierce motifs, offering both a warning and an invitation to those who dared to explore further.

Passing through the city the traveller accounted for each one, creating a mental inventory. On the other side of the city across the river, the same knocker was to be observed, interesting, the traveller thought, as it matched with one they saw earlier. But as the traveller continued on their meanders they again found another that matched a previous knocker. The traveller wondered, there was almost a pull or a slight hum that came from the pairs they've witnessed. Something beckoned them to knock, the traveller, all too easily, gave into temptation and delicately lifted the brass handle that called. This one, a ring split in two up the middle. Each side morphed into a wolf-like creature with feline eyes and teeth, mirroring one another. Three times the traveller knocked, echoing down the now empty street, all that lingered now was the slight morning mist, pierced by a starting sunrise. There was an unidentifiable pull from the door, a wind that urged them towards the cold brass knocker.

After a few moments of silence the traveller took a careful step back onto the cobbled streets, but at the instance they began to turn away a slight movement caught in the corner of their vision halted the traveller's turn. The door, silent without a creak, had so subtly opened a slither. Reaching out a hand the traveller cautiously tapped a finger to the door. It fell open with ease. All that the traveller could make out were darkened shadows in a hallway of sorts. The wind, as if an usherer of the house, gently nudged them toward the entrance. Filled with curiosity and a slight tremor they entered the threshold into the hallway. One foot in front of the other the traveller clambered over hallway clutter into further shadows. Upon turning their head back it was too late for the traveller to realise that the door closing on its hinges would block out their remaining light. A brief retrace of steps toward the door, the traveller reached for the handle to unlock. It was no use. As stiff as the statues who watched the streets.

Maybe there would be another exit somewhere. The only other way out was back through the hallway, or so they'd hope. The faint outline of black against a darker grey was all the warning they had of objects to dodge through this route. With each step into the darkness, a shiver of apprehension coursed through the traveller's veins, their mind racing with questions and uncertainties. The sound of a metal bucket rattling off concrete flooring, echoing into the abyss had the traveller jump, knocking into more objects that clattered. The harsh noise hurried the traveller to move further forward toward where the wind encouraged. The continuous chaos caused from their cautiousness only increased the traveller's need to escape from this dark tunnel of dread they found themself in.

As the reality of their situation dawned upon them, panic tightened its grip around the traveller's chest, their breaths coming in shallow gasps. Every corner turned seemed to lead them further into the labyrinth of their own making, a maze of shadows and echoes that whispered of ancient secrets.

Their face came to face with a solid wall that halted them in an abrupt stop. The traveller steadily ran their hands up the glossed wood or what felt like wood, and found a cold doorknob to their right side. It was another door. Twisting and pulling they were met with light, daylight. Pushing themself forward they walked out onto a street, not the street they previously were.

They must have exited at the other side of the building as it seemed like a fair enough distance to put it down to that.

They turned as they heard the creak of the door and watched it close behind them with a slick click and a lock. This door differed in size from the one they entered but with the same knocker. A pairing. In the detail of the character's faces, their features slightly askew, elicited a knowing and playful look as if they shared a secret with the traveller.

Shaking the strange feeling off with the rounding of their shoulders, they took in the surroundings of this unfamiliar street. Through the bustle of city-goers they hoped to navigate somewhere they could get their bearings back.

With each unfamiliar sight that greeted them, the traveller's mind raced to make sense of their surroundings, seeking solace in familiarity amidst the chaos of the unknown. They were in the same city, its language spoken by the same lampposts, flaked-painted walls and delicately detailed rafters of overhung roofs. Yet, every street corner revealed new mysteries, each alleyway a doorway to uncharted territory.

As the streets guided them inexorably forward, the traveller's footsteps quickened with a mix of trepidation and curiosity. Eventually, they emerged into a square. The scene before them was hauntingly familiar, reminiscent of images they had studied and dreamed of visiting. However, a jolt of realisation coursed through them as they realised that this square lay across the city, far from the location where they had entered the first doorway.

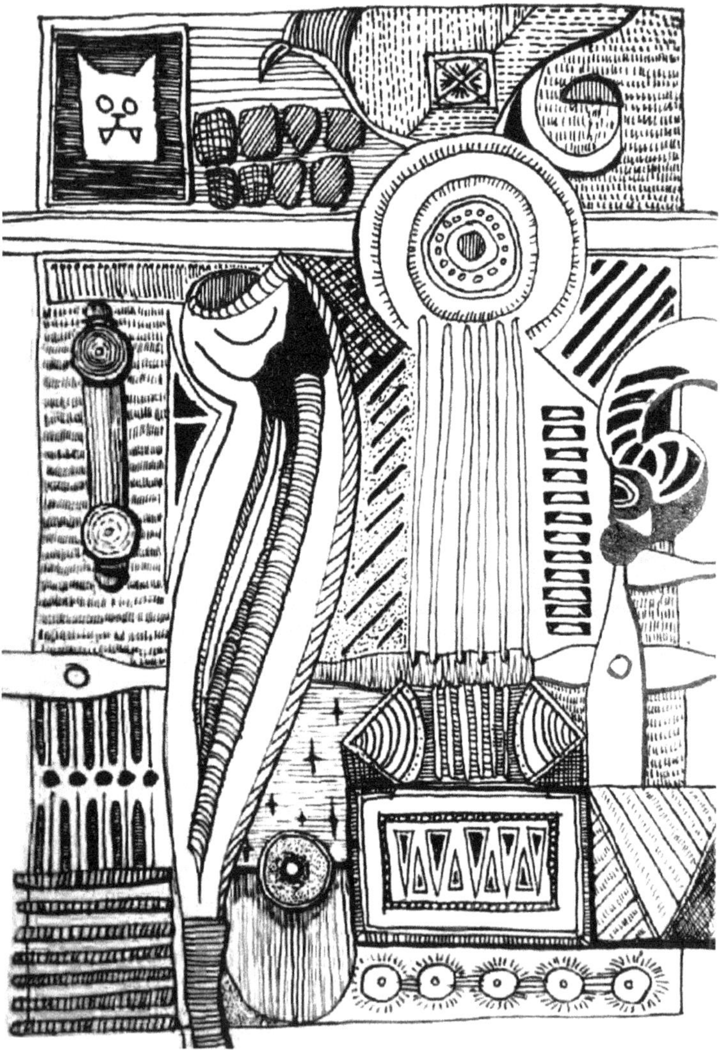

Engravings of Memory Architects

There was a pattern in places, what the traveller saw was repeated again by others. Ghosted memories layered themselves in space. As an observer of that same place, memories of strangers' ghosts lingered, with the first memory of that place likely setting the precedent.

Patterns emerged, each step leaving an imprint on memory. What the traveller witnessed was a script, enacted by strangers who, in their transient presence, contributed to the narrative of place. These initial impressions acted as the architects of recollection, setting the stage for subsequent encounters.

As the observer of these unfolding scenes, the traveller became a curator of ghosted memories, layers of past interactions that lingered in the present. A city corner, for instance, transformed with each visit — a couple immersed in conversation, another pair sharing a coffee and cigarette, and yet another trio engaged in animated discussion. These individuals, seemingly disconnected, were united by the common thread of the traveller's gaze.

Segments of cityscape upon each return to familiar spaces invited a comparison to the initial encounter, a reflective journey through the ghosted memories that shaped the traveller's perception of the city.

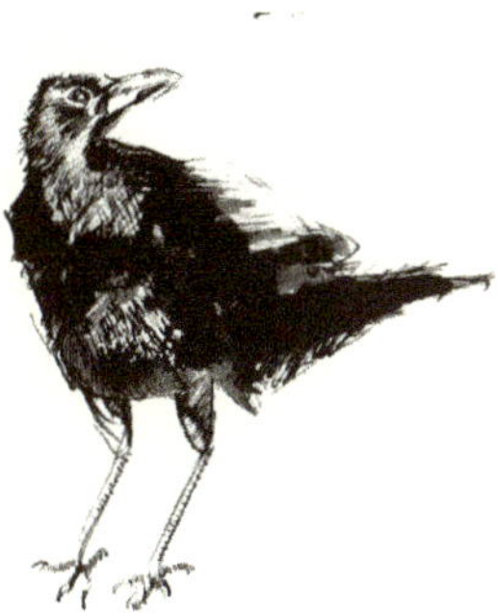

Picnic between a Traveller and Crow

After failing to locate a spot free of littered cigarette butts, the traveller accepted where they sat on the clearing of grass. On the bank by the edge of the city, they lay down their jumper so that dried prickly grass would not irritate where they rested. Others were stopped there too, lying, basking in the sun. The traveller was looking forward to their prepared picnic since they had set off on this beautiful day. They unpacked their boxes and wrappings in an arranged order in front of them. They wanted to take a moment of peaceful solitude, closing their eyes to feel the sun warming their skin, listening to the paddling strokes of rowers and the last of autumn leaves shimmering as they fell from their branches.

A crunch and a rustle disrupted the peaceful ambiance, prompting the traveller to open their eyes. To their sur-

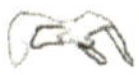

prise, a crow hopped toward them on both feet, eyeing the picnic laid out before them.

The crow, with its sleek black feathers and intelligent eyes, approached confidently. With a caw, it opened its beak and made a request, "What can I give you in return for sharing your lunch?" The traveller, slightly alarmed but intrigued, responded, "How about a story? If it's good enough, I'll gladly share my sandwich with you."

The crow, seemingly satisfied with the proposition, perched nearby, ready to unfold its tale. With a mischievous glint in its eye, the crow began to recount a story of a city divided by a river, two separate worlds unified by bridges and woven together into a harmonious whole. As the crow narrated the tale, the traveller found themself animated by the bird's storytelling.

"In this city, a river winds its way, dividing the landscape like a wound that has become stitched together by bridges over time. The city, once split in two, has evolved and grown, its very nature shaped by the flow of the river and the stories it carries.

"Imagine, long ago, two distinct cities residing on either side of the river. Neither part was aware of what it once was. The people living their lives in their own worlds, unaware of the wonders across the water. Then, one day, someone embarked on a journey by boat, discovering the beauty and vitality of the opposite side. The excitement was contagious, and soon, inhabitants from both sides were sharing tales of their respective halves.

"As more boats traversed the river, the love for each side blossomed. Eventually, the decision was made to build a bridge, a permanent connection to bind the two cities into one. The stitches of the bridge closed the wound, and now, there is no trace of the division that once existed. The cities merged into a harmonious whole, their unique histories now blending seamlessly.

"The river is the onlooker to the cityscape's evolution, observing the growth and transformation of the city it bisects. The bridges not only connect the two sides but also provide those who venture across with a split view of each city side when passing over the connections, offering glimpses of the hillsides and beyond."

Upon the story's conclusion, the crow fixed its gaze on the traveller, awaiting judgement. The traveller, thoroughly entertained, couldn't help but smile. "Well done, feathered storyteller," they remarked, handing over a seeded half of their sandwich to share with the clever crow. The traveller at the city's edge, glanced down the river, remarking on the many bridges that stitched each side together. The river gently drifted, and for a moment, the two shared a peaceful exchange of food and stories by the water's edge.

Night's Illusion, Day's Revelation

Once embraced by the golden radiance of candlelit flames, the streets resonated with a buzzing, humming glow that extended beyond the reach of flickering flames. Along the water, those lights mapped the traveller's route, creating a pathway that, from a distance, concealed the formation of streets. By day, those lights served as ornamental accents, adorning heavy-bricked facades. Some clung intimately to the buildings, while others stretched out like gentlemen holding umbrellas, offering the wandering traveller a token of light.

In the cloak of night, those warm, buttery lights cast an inviting glow, creating an illusion of a warmer night than reality allowed. Found in large sets across the city, they formed constellations of illumination. The metal components of the street lamps exhibited beautifully crafted character—metal twisted, curved, and cast with a variety that, while always clustered in the same locations, made it easier to identify their location. The craftsmanship carried distinguishable accents, a reflection of the city's variations.

During the day, the lights slumbered, and the metal structures stood exposed. Details emerged more prominently, revealing the material's identity—typically crafted from iron or aluminium. Some were adorned with the flaky texture of rust; a kiss of time, while others boasted a thick, glossy coat of black paint, a shield against corrosion. In the evening glow, shadows took centre stage, outlining uneven placements and casting cloaks of black shadows. These daytime nuances became a silent challenge for the traveller, causing more stumbles without the guiding nightlights highlighting the wonky way forward.

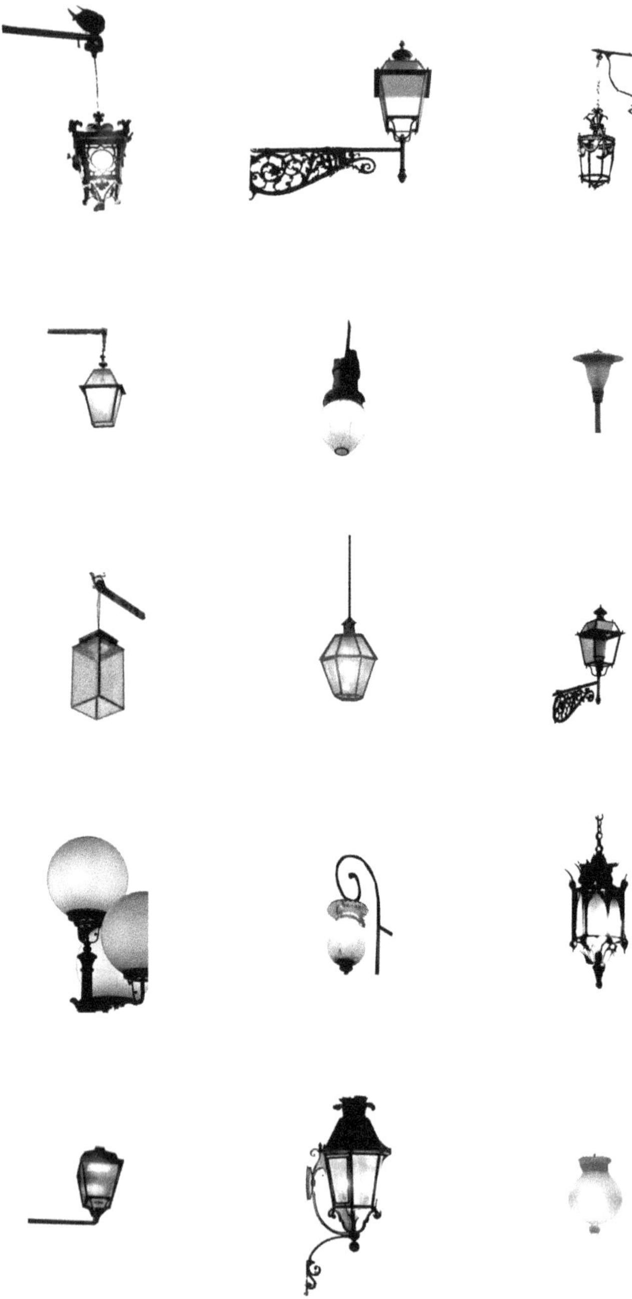

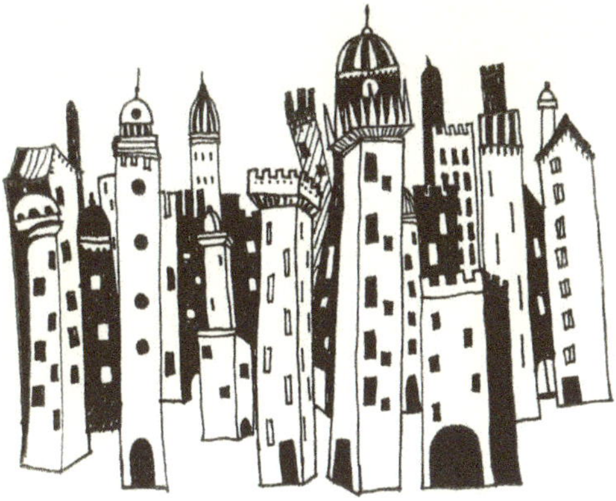

Skies of Stone and Memory

Sitting in an establishment, the traveller noticed that upside-down coffee cups were stacked concerningly high above the coffee machine by the window. The structures, upon first glance, reminded them of a miniature city, one they had heard of before, with some stacks too high, creating worry about its stability. They knew this tale from another city, where only a couple of towers remained. The two towers that persisted told tales of a time when the skyline was crowded with vertical structures that from a distance, travellers would believe to be a forest of stone.

In the modern gaze, these towers stood as watchmen, remnants of a once sprawling arboretum of urbanity. The taller tower, a beacon that stretched skyward, now captured the attention of each passerby, a lone survivor amid the four to five-story blocks it neighboured.

However, in centuries past, locals strolling through the city were not met with the same spectacle. The towers were not isolated landmarks demanding uplifted gazes. Instead, they were companions, rising like trees in a city that grew upward rather than outward. These turrets of brown brick, devoid of leaves, had an uncanny uniformity. Each tower boasted its four corners, all reaching a similar height, prompting one to wonder—were they trying to match each other's lofty aspirations?

Picture a city where these towers weren't mere structures but homes, where neighbours in high towers exchanged waves, peering down on the moving life below. This was a city of stalagmites, appearing to have grown organically from the earth. At its zenith, a staggering 180 towers punctuated the skyline, each one a unique entity in both purpose and design. Some served as dwellings, others as prisons or shops, and a few as vantage points over the city.

Yet, time took its toll, decay set in. The towering stalwarts, once proud and erect, succumbed to the wear of weather and the burden of their own existence. One by one, these stone sentinels fell, leaving only a scattering of remnants to tell the tale of what once was.

And so, in the present day, the two remaining towers stood as witnesses to a city's evolution, its past etched in stone and sky, standing with ghosts.

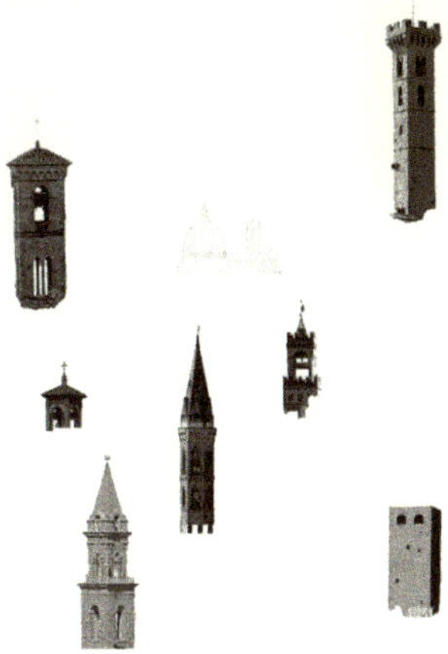

Barter of Observations

Nestled upon the hilltop, the climb was rewarded by tranquillity. Distant echoes of car engines became softened by the chimes of leaves whispering as they brushed by in the wind. After some moments, nature's silence of the city broke from the passage of a train a few slopes down. The traveller's gaze swept back up to their ascent, from the park's seats, thin iron gates and passed the tracks they had now noticed. A glass theatre of windows with white ornate columns was tucked into a perimeter of narrow trees, protecting the structure from gales. The traveller marvelled at their view, looking down at rooftops but wishing for a magnifier to offer a closer look at the intricacies of the spires, tiles and chimneys. Following the path and the sets of symmetrical steps back, the traveller studied their immediate surroundings. Down at their feet, cascading, a gentle rain of pine needles upon the sloping ground fell where they found their seat.

Upon their spot a grand dome commanded the centre of the traveller's vision, it guided gazes exploring the surroundings. It was a place that demanded attention, a pause where the world momentarily faded away. The cool breeze offered respite from the heat, if only for a fleeting moment, while nearby benches provided silent companionship.

Their eyes shifted to the couple on the adjacent bench, their shared moment a stark contrast to the introspective solitude they now wore. The juxtaposition of their togetherness and the traveller's isolation sparked a quiet contemplation. Just as the thought of loneliness began to settle, a raindrop landed gently on their cheek, a subtle reminder of the world's attempt to reach out to touch emotions.

Here, on this precipice between city bustle and natural calm, they observed the graceful flight of pigeons from the river's edge to their side, arcs mirroring their contemplative state. Writing became a joy in this city, in this very spot. With a pen in hand, there was no need to move; they captured the essence of the world with every stroke. Yet, they were but a traveller passing through. Was the city granting them this experience, or were they, in turn, giving something back? A barter of time and experience, perhaps, an intimate exchange that only the keen observer comprehends.

In the vast expanse above, points punctuated the sky, and domes reached towards infinity without disrupting the serenity. They attempted to count them, but the task proved elusive, frustration mounting until they abandoned the game. Attention drew elsewhere, much like a magpie captivated by a gleaming object. The traveller imagined themself as this curious creature, taking flight, swooping down from the pine tree, only to realise the object was larger than life itself. A metaphorical echo, a reminder that some experiences are too immense to be captured, even by the most observant traveller.

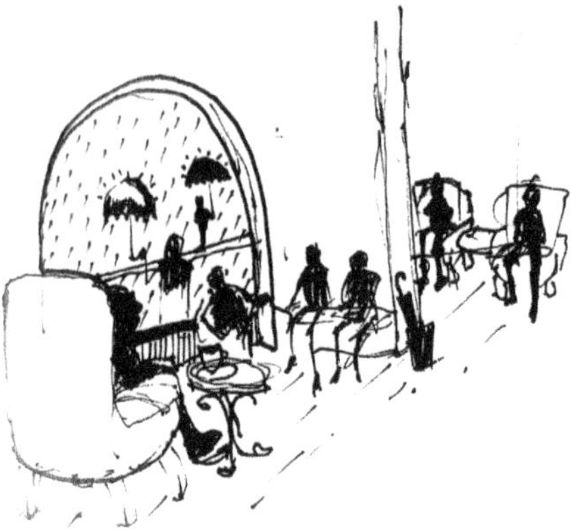

When Time Takes Shelter

Seated in the café, the traveller found themself unexpectedly tethered to the moment, the external world intruding upon their intended adventure. The traveller's gaze shifted from the raindrops splattering against the window to the growing numbers of patrons seeking refuge from the downpour. Crinkled ponchos clung to bodies, promising a damp discomfort the traveller was glad to avoid. The entrance's floor was exposed to the weather's intrusion, the air now carrying a different quality, heavy with the scent of wetness and an anticipation.

Any drink would suffice in this moment of waiting. Some patrons lingered near the door, as if hoping for the rain to relent, but it seemed the storm had decided to stay a while longer, forcing an unspoken agreement among the couple in the entryway. Their silent nod acknowledged the inevitable truth: they would be staying here longer than they had planned.

The traveller couldn't help but think about the irony of the situation. Earlier, in the throes of their exploration, they had thirsted for water. Now, in the form of weather, they only wished the rain away.

Water was indeed wonderful. It had become that time of year when the morning walks along the main streets revealed vaporous clouds gathering over the trees that shaded the roads. The once warm hues of the buildings were de-saturated by the grey, bringing a welcomed coolness to the air.

In this capsulated instance they favoured their teacup, unique to other establishments. Awkward in its form to pick up with a single hand and sip, but perfect for two hands to wrap around. They leaned back in their seat, cosy in warmth and comfort.

City and Contours of Transition

From the depths of the valley, where the hum of machines intertwined with the rhythms of nature, the traveller embarked on a journey, following the winding path that led to the peak. They favoured the sunlit side initially, basking in the warm glow, but as the journey progressed, the outskirts of the valley came into view, and the traveller crossed over, seeking the comforting shade as the sun's intensity grew, their breaths becoming staggered, and beads of perspiration trickling down their back.

In these outskirts, houses embraced more generous gardens, and the calls of birds became more apparent, a melodic contrast to the distant hum of city machines. The transition from the city centre to these suburbs was palpable, the character of the place becoming distinguishable. Amidst this changing landscape stood a gothic house, its presence a vibrant peach complimenting the blue of the sky.

This gothic house became a memorable node in the traveller's journey, a place the companion had suggested they capture, even though no camera accompanied them on that walk. Instead, the traveller relied on their senses, committing the details to memory. They observed the dark lace-like underhang that protected the roof, a striking contrast against the orange-coated exterior. It seemed to blend seamlessly with the encroaching autumnal ambiance that hung in the air that day, as the city fell away, giving way to pockets of nature merging seamlessly with the countryside.

Their hurried footsteps crunched paper-like leaves beneath, a reminder of the shifting seasons, as they hastened to catch the changing light of the day. Winding streets unfolded into wider access roads, revealing the wonders of this transitional space where urban life gracefully met the serenity of nature. Each step enriched the traveller's journey, a seamless blend of urban exploration and the embrace of natural beauty, etching a vivid picture in their mind's eye.

Internal Landscape of Silent Musings

In the soft glow of the night, the muse would often find themself lost in contemplation through the window pane, a cigarette hanging languidly between their fingers. Smoke curled around them in this ritual, a moment of contemplation before they retreated. The traveller, too, would occasionally join them, their intimate moments unfolding against the backdrop of the abode's garden, which, in those moments, became theirs alone. It was a peculiar garden, resembling a balcony in size but with nothing to look down on, only up to the sky or through gaps in the gating to the neighbour's assortments of pots and plants. The only time the traveller ventured outside there in the night was only with the muse.

In the evening's dim light, the muse transformed into flickers of light within the shadows. They sat there, framed by the soft glow of the room, a silhouette against the darkness outside. Their gaze would drift through the glass, yet not quite register on the scene before them. It was as though they looked but did not look, their thoughts far away, transported to another realm. The traveller observed them through the physical pane of glass, but the muse's gaze was veiled by an internal barrier, mind wandering to places unknown.

The traveller was intrigued, a curiosity kindled by the enigmatic depths of the muse's thoughts. There was a desire to pry, to unravel the mystery that lay beneath those distant eyes. Yet, amidst the poetic silence of those moments, the traveller hesitated. There was something profoundly poetic in leaving the muse's musings unread, in preserving the sanctity of their secrets. It was as if their internal landscape, as mysterious and elusive as it was, added an ethereal layer to their connection, a bond made from shared intimacy and unspoken mysteries. And so, the traveller chose to cherish the enigma, allowing the muse's thoughts to remain their own, adding a touch of magic to the quiet nights they spent together.

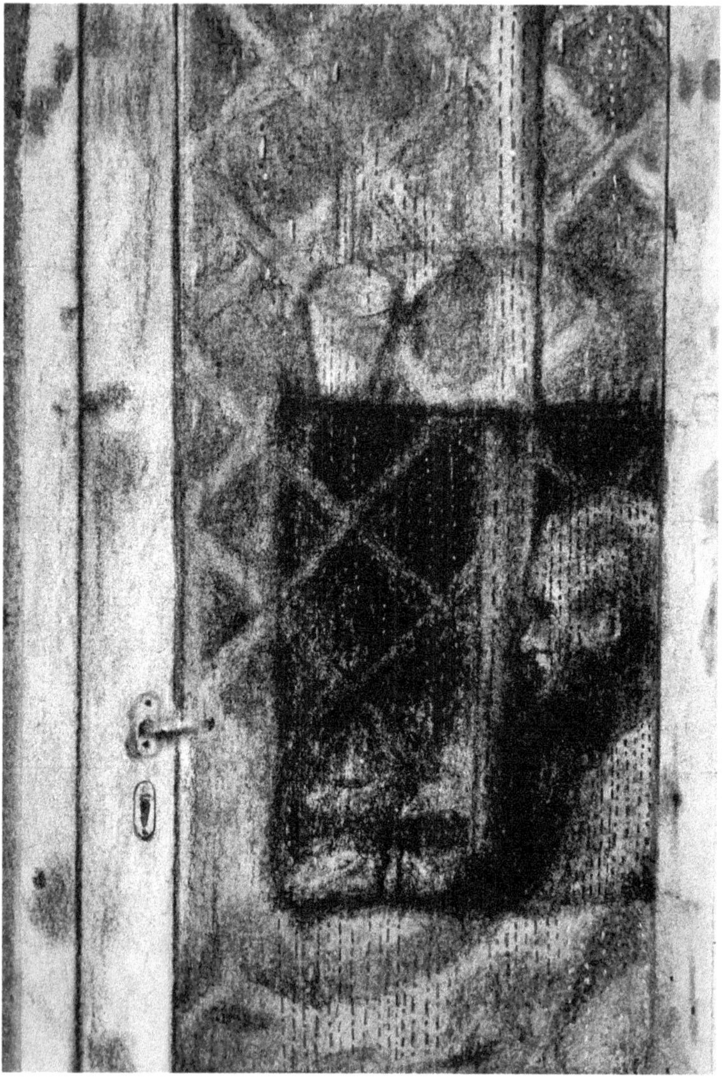

A Tower's Night Tale

Perched high between two gentle hills, a solitary tower extended its hand towards the city below. The hillsides, adorned in soft yellows and creams with terracotta roofs, cascaded downward, revealing winding paths that snaked through the verdant slopes. As the traveller walked from their city's centre northward at night, they saw the neighbouring city as starlight in the skies, becoming a constellation of city lights. Street lamps and windows formed patterns reminiscent of celestial arrangements, a terrestrial constellation mapping the contours of the land.

Enchanted by this distant vista, the traveller found solace in the harmony of man-made constellations and the allure of the night. Having visited there now, its point became a new marker on their memory map, adding a new layer to this personal constellation, making the night sky a celestial roadmap of their travels and the stories etched into the landscapes they've explored.

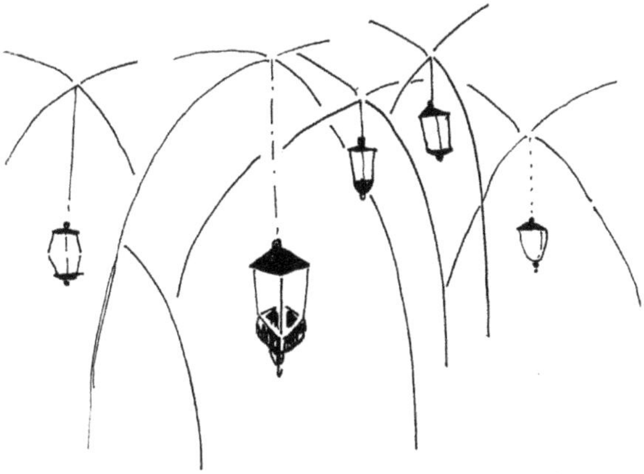

Keystones of Light

A subtle delicacy could be observed in certain transition points from streets into shelters' entrances. Where arches gracefully curved overhead, a three-dimensional spectacle unfolded. The arches, forming rib vaults, intersected in lines, converging at a central point. Here, a radiant jewel suspended from an intricate chain of metal orchestrated the architectural composition.

The glow emanating from the suspended light served as the keystone, seamlessly binding the elements into a harmonious whole. Without this luminescent touch, one might have imagined the structure unravelling, the arcs losing their poise, and the entire framework at the precipice of collapse. This was the fine consideration of architecture, where light became the unseen force, the poet of the grandeur of design.

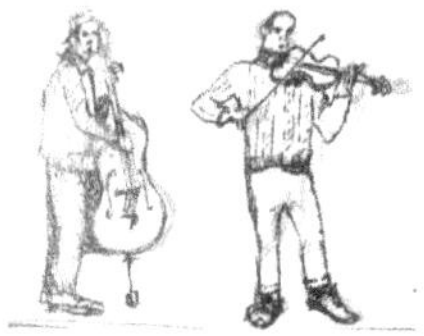

Passage Through the Crowded Throng

The crowded streets closed in, a sea of shuffle and scuffle,
Narrowing spaces or just more people to ruffle.
Stuck in a rut, the traveller tutted with dismay,
Feeling the stress of needing to reach their way.

But wait, what was that sound, music drawing near?
Two men to the side, instruments they rear.
One with a cello, stepped forward with a hello,
The other, with a fiddle, presented a riddle to clear.

"If solved, we'll play our music, a lively tune,
Swift-paced for footsteps to dance and swoon.
The traveller can then proceed,
To their destination, unimpeded."

"Give me your riddle," the traveller asserted,
The man with the fiddle grinned, excitement in his eyes spinned.

"I'm always in front, never left behind,
Stretching far and wide, yet not confined.
Marked by footsteps, yet not a shoe,
Travelling through me, discoveries anew.
What am I?" The traveller pondered, a street full of strife,
As the crowded space leaned on panic and life.

After a moment, the traveller leaned in close,
Whispered the answer, the riddle's repose.
The man lifted his fiddle, a joyful tease,
With the cello in tune, the crowd started to ease.

Swaying and moving, the path became clear,
The traveller continued their journey with cheer.

In the Embrace of Conversations

A concealed haven, tucked away south of the river just beyond the west bridge, the café's expansive arch windows went unnoticed unless viewed from across the street. Throughout the day, intellectual discussions and collaborative projects unfolded within its walls, gradually dispersing until the last scholar yawned, packing up their musings.

As daylight faded and the bar took the spotlight, diligent studiers were politely asked to pair up, making room for the evening crowd. The eclectic interior, a modern twist on a grandmother's house, featured starkly colored walls and a vivid mural of red and black trees climbing two floors.

Venturing upstairs, the traveller discovered two spots—one more furtive than the other. Opting for the less frequented corner, they settled on a corner bench by the arched window. The wooden floorboards betrayed the anxious wobble of a fellow patron's foot, creating minute but distracting ripples in their coffee.

While engrossed in their studies, the enticing aroma of the gentleman's food became a sensory tease. The man seated closest to the window sparked an unexpected interaction, posing a question in his native tongue. Stammering through their lack of comprehension, the traveller managed to convey their linguistic limitations. His understanding smile preceded a request to watch over his belongings during a brief bathroom break—a fleeting connection in the orchestrated set of the café.

Observing the bar staff revealed their choreographed movements, conveying messages through tone, expressions, and hushed conversations. Later, as the night progressed and the lemon-infused alcohol took effect, the traveller found themself engaged in conversations that went beyond language barriers.

If they were to revisit this city, the café would undoubtedly exert a magnetic pull. A place where the aroma of coffee, the vibrancy of the staff, and the fleeting nature of encounters converged, leaving an indelible mark on the traveller's soul.

City's Balcony

A nightly ritual, rain or storm, saw someone perched at this precipice. It resembled an open-air theatre on warm evenings with gentle winds. The journey began by heading south over the bridge, then eastward, following the surging crowd moving like a colony of ants. Swaying S's of roads guided the traveller past city walls and ornate fountains with golden oranges swimming in their turquoise depths. Along this route, caution was advised of the merchant with paintings laid on the path, hoping for an unfortunate passerby to accidentally step on the artwork and demand payment. Almost at the top, the crowds loomed above as the path ascended to the pinnacle. Stalls offering refreshing beverages, surprisingly at a reasonable price, anchored their thirst with a purchase.

Arriving half an hour before the sun began to set was

essential to secure their chosen seats on the steps. Overlooking the city, its bridges, and the river disappeared into the hills. From this vantage point, a neighbouring city and isolated houses on steep hilltops were visible, highlighted by the soft glow of facades. The formal steps, like a concrete hillside, hosted musicians who casually played the crowds with melodies that set the backdrop for an evening ahead. Seated there, watching the horizon set ablaze, be it with a friend, companion, loved one, or alone, each experience was memorable and distinct. Scenes unfolded — a blue shirt, red shoes set bold by green grapes, a pizza and beer, a breath of solitude. Each encounter owned its unique state, different from the last, yet this space connected the encounters and stories, tying memories together. As the sun set, the curtain fell, concluding this captivating cinematic experience.

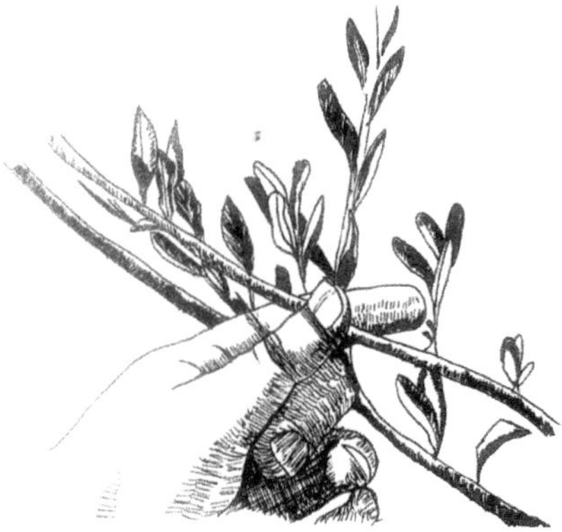

A Lovers' Olive Odyssey

While the specifics of their faces eluded memory, the details lingered in tactile impressions; the cable-knit texture of a grey jumper, the worn denim of jeans.

In the eyes of a sun-drenched day, the scene unfolded like a series of carefully curated images, akin to the tender transitions in silent films. The golden rays of morning warmth permeated through thin sheets, casting a nostalgic glow on the lovers strolling along a seemingly endless road that stretched outward from the city.

In the traveller's mind, this path was more than a walk—it was a linear journey, a narrative corridor of shared moments.

Hand in hand, the lovers exchanged gestures, their affection manifesting in subtle and gentle touches. The road, elevated above groves, allowed them to pluck ripe olives directly from the branches if they so wished. Warm and slightly rough hands delicately swung a branch, revealing an insect camouflaged as a red cherry—a charming discovery amidst this olive tree. Glossy paper-like leaves adorned their branches, catching and reflecting the sun's rays as they disappeared into the distance, beyond rounded hills and clear blue skies.

As they walked, a memory of music, the rustle of leaves in the wind, the constant stopped scuffles and starts of footsteps, the whispering melodies of nature extending past the olive groves.

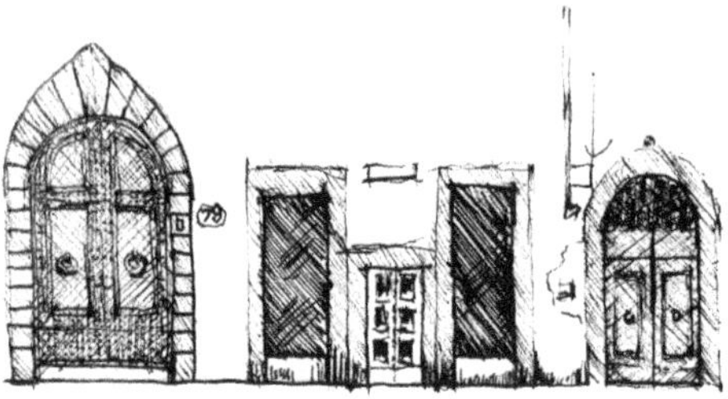

Shifting Perspectives by Wandering Left

As the traveller grew more familiar with the city, a comforting sense of routine began to take hold. The daily journey to the favourite café unfolded with practised ease, guided by well-worn paths. The traveller's steps consistently fell on the same side of the street, a choice deemed quickest, most efficient, and fastest. However, a memory resurfaced of the traveller's early days in the city when uncertainty led them to traverse the opposite side, with numerous crossings to find their way.

On the route from the northern quarters to the city centre, the traveller habitually aligned with the right side of the street. Their gaze rarely drifted to the left, as their attention was captivated by the ornate doorways and fine details that adorned the right side of the road. There seemed to be no compelling reason to divert their attention leftward. Yet, on a day when a companion joined them, they took the lead, and a subtle shift occurred. The traveller now found themself on the left side of the street, offering a different perspective of their well-trodden path. The change, although just a few metres, felt somewhat disconcerting. The traveller's accustomed comfort zone was now exposed to the passersby on the other side, obscuring their view of the familiar details on the right.

Such is the nature of habits and familiarity; they are easily disrupted, like the gentle ripple in the river when the egret takes flight from the water's edge. Even the slightest alteration can stir a sense of discomfort, yet it's in these moments of change that often discover new perspectives and hidden details, enriching connection to the city and its ever-evolving stories.

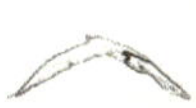

Laughter of Languages

As the traveller hurried down the street, their pace matched that of an elderly lady ahead. Her petite figure hung a yellow buttoned cardigan and a thin, ruby scarf, her slip-on leather shoes tapping lightly against the pavement. Having lived in the city for some time, the traveller had grown accustomed to the rhythm of daily strolls, often blending in seamlessly with the locals.

It wasn't uncommon for the traveller to be mistaken for a resident from time to time. On this particular day, as they found themself gaining on the elderly lady, a subtle exchange unfolded. Sensing the traveller's need to overtake, the lady chuckled and made a comment. Though the words were unintelligible, the traveller responded with a laugh, understanding the implication about their brisk pace.

The laughter served as the common language, an invitation for further interaction. The elderly lady, encouraged by the traveller's response, continued to speak, unaware that her words were not understood. Despite the traveller's inability to converse in the local language, they shared a moment of connection through shared amusement.

However, as the conversation carried on, the traveller realised they couldn't sustain the facade. With a sense of disappointment, they quickened their pace, eager to escape the awkwardness of a conversation in a language they didn't comprehend. Yet, even as they hurried away, the sound of the elderly lady's laughter lingered in the air.

Shelved Perspectives from the Escarpment

In the environs lying beyond the city's central precincts, the placement of architecture assumed a distinct character within the rugged terrain. As the traveller ascended the undulating paths, their footsteps grew weighty with each incline, until the gradients verged upon near-verticality, prompting a lateral transition as the pathways meandered from left to right.

In this gradual ascent, the domiciles harmonised with the topography, appearing as stacks akin to shelves upon which the city's peripheral dwellings rested. Seated upon one such shelf, the traveller assumed the role of a passive observer, surveying the city's tableau below with a sense of detached curiosity, reminiscent of a scholar perusing the shelves of an expansive library.

From this elevated vantage point, beyond the immediate confines of this urban emporium, the traveller's gaze fell, then extended toward the rooftops where the cityscape converged with the verdant expanse of surrounding foliage, marking the boundary between civilization and the untamed wilderness.

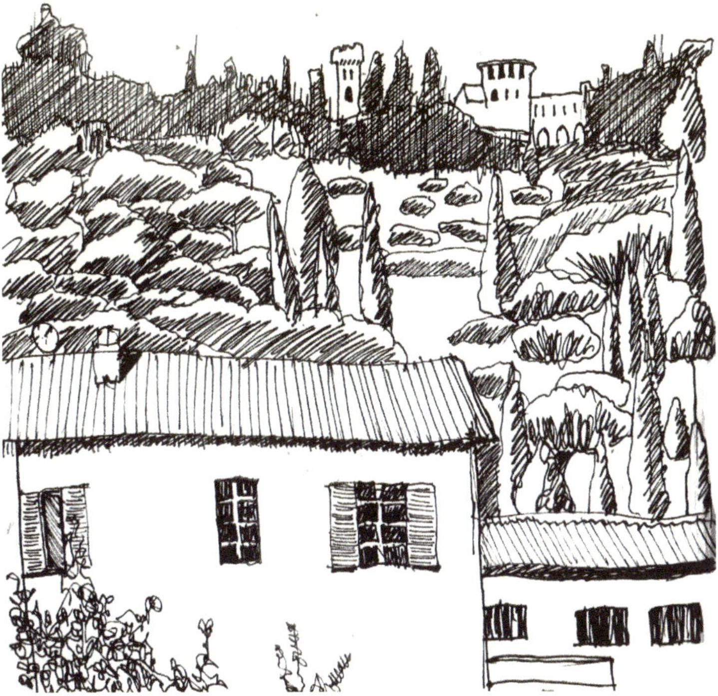

Glimpses Through Gates

The building had coyly hidden behind its gate, a silent observer to the crossroads the traveller passed every day. It lingered in the corner of the eye, unnoticed until the stir of activity outside drew the traveller's attention. The texture of the gate overlaid the delicate facade, half-shielding the building like a secretive veil. It transformed into a stencil, crafting small windows and eyelets, tempting curious glances to peer through.

This structure was artfully tucked away from the main street, yet its gate aligned seamlessly, providing a sense of continuity with its surroundings. Without the gate, the space between the building and the street would have stretched openly, devoid of privacy. However, this lace of architectural decor had acted as a boundary line, delicately separating the vibrancy of city life from the undisturbed homestead within. The building, veiled behind the gate, had become a mysterious enclave, its secrets hidden from the hurried gaze of passersby.

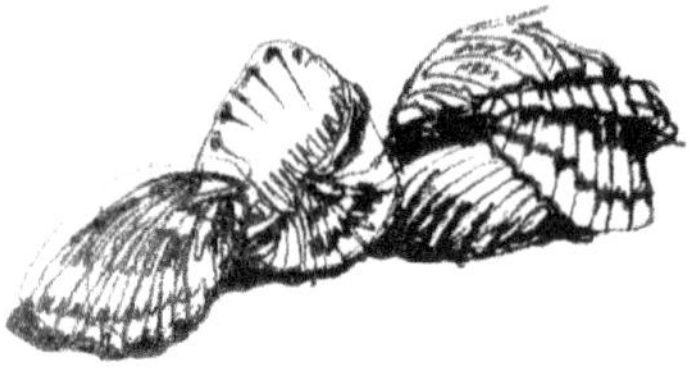

Exchanges of Transient Tokens

In the fading light of the beach day, with the sands empty and the waves crashing gently nearby, the traveller reclined on sandy beach towels, sipping water warmed by the sun, with their companion by their side. Not far away, a man dipped and rose along the water's edge, a snorkel in his mouth and goggles covering his eyes, diligently searching for treasure beneath the waves. There was a sense of anticipation mixed with worry as the traveller wondered where he would emerge next, his direction often surprising them by veering away from their expectations. When he finally surfaced, his presence became an anchor, carefully treading over the sand, pushing it through his feet as he approached.

Beads of sea salt water clung to his skin, which had taken on an almost Sienna burnt hue from the sun. With a warm smile, he greeted the traveller and extended his arms, cradling carefully, he opened his hands like a book to unveil a collection of shells in opened palms. Words in an unfamiliar tongue flowed from his lips, the meaning of his words escaping the traveller, but the gesture was universal. The shells he presented, striped with hues of yellow, white, and oranges, encapsulated the essence of that day, the warmth of the sun, and the sincerity of the gift. The traveller was surprised and touched; these shells were for them. Gratefully, they conveyed their thanks as he walked away to gather his belongings and then disappeared into the horizon, leaving them with the precious exchange. They were more than gifts; they were fragments of a fleeting connection, a gesture that meant more than words.

Later, the traveller examined each shell closely, noting the subtle differences in size and slight variations in colour between them. From a distance, they all appeared the same, reminiscent of a childhood memory when they would admire the jewellery in their mother's box, appreciating the beauty in each piece. This memory became a jewel tucked away, ready to be rediscovered whenever they encountered similar shells, eliciting a shy smile on their lips, a reminder of that fleeting yet meaningful encounter with their companion and the old man by the sea.

City Plumage

In the traveller's months of meandering through the city's carved streets, a vivid mental image emerged—a sectional drawing capturing the birds perched on various spots—the riverbanks, lampposts, and walls. Birds, resilient and adaptable, landing gracefully on anything in their path, became indelible marks in the traveller's memories.

The city's residents, accustomed to these feathered visitors, seldom raised an eyebrow when a bird fluttered by in the distance. Their presence was as common as the cobblestones beneath their feet. Yet, on a particular day by the river, amidst the backdrop of tightly packed, tall, and brilliantly coloured buildings, a significant shift occurred.

Tourists, usually engrossed in capturing the picturesque scenery, turned their attention to an unexpected guest. A lone goose, regal in its stance, graced the river's wall where people gathered for photographs. With only one leg, it stood tall and proud in resilience. Its plumage, a vibrant mosaic of colours, drew the eye, capturing the attention of all who beheld it. Clean and immaculate, it seemed almost otherworldly against the city's historic backdrop.

In that moment, it was as though a pair of scissors had been taken to the string of street movement, breaking its usual and consistent flow. The city's pulse slowed, as the creature itself had taken centre stage. The juxtaposition of the elegant goose against repetitive narrow dwellings created a scene worthy of remembrance. It reflected coexistence of the city's human inhabitants and the wild creatures that graced its streets and rivers. A scene etched into the traveller's mind's eye.

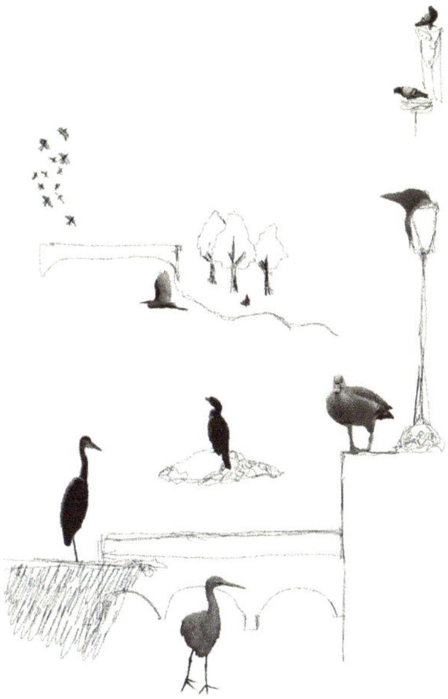

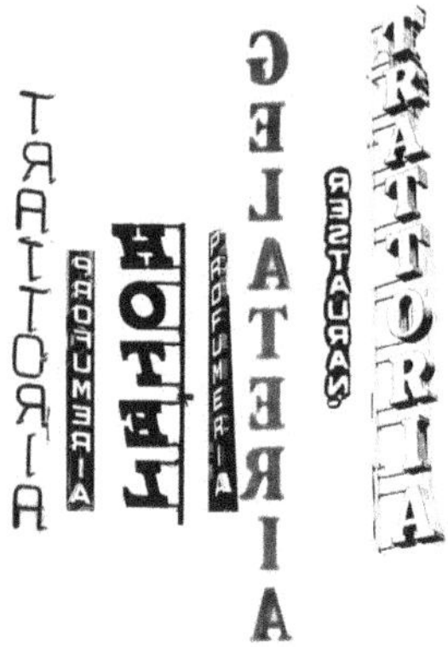

Lighthouses in the Night

Entering the city centre, unmistakable signs announced the traveller's arrival: the city signs, illuminated and vibrant, hung from buildings like lettered lighthouses guiding the way. Each letter, carefully crafted, fell below the next, their words a mesmerising blend of familiarity and novelty, capturing the traveller's attention with their whimsical back-to-front charm.

These captivating signs were a hallmark of active establishments, especially those of the beverage and gourmet variety. Fonts, meticulously chosen, bore the delicate touch of decorative serifs and an upright posture, standing tall and proud. When illuminated by the warm glow of light, these signs beckoned life, almost audible in the hum of excitement that surrounded them. They invited the passersby with an irresistible charm, drawing them in like moths to a flame, promising an experience that surpassed the ordinary.

In this illuminated spectacle, life found its rhythm. The buzz emanating from these signs mirrored the vivacity of the city itself, creating an atmosphere that crackled with energy and anticipation. Each flickering light became a star in the city's night sky, guiding wanderers and seekers alike to the heart of the action.

Their presence on the cityscape was not just a matter of practicality but a lace of meticulous artistry and attention to detail that embellished the city's cultural form. These signs were not merely symbols; they were storytellers, weaving tales of elaborate evenings and quiet rendezvous. They were the embodiment of an identity carefully crafted, a stew of tradition and modernity simmering in the city's cauldron. With each flicker and glow, they spoke narratives of engaging evenings, whispered conversations, and culinary delights that lingered on the palate long after the meal had concluded.

In their glow, the traveller found familiarity and the promise of new discoveries, for in the city, where there was light, there was indeed life.

A Pilgrimage to the Serpent and Crab

The traveller found themself once more embarking on an exploration, navigating through a grand square where the perimeter was adorned with arcades. In this locale, an architectural wonder transported the traveller to another city, one previously visited, where every street was sheltered with arcades resembling the sinuous form of a winding serpent. Over time, some of these arcades had tilted towards the roadside, inducing a mental wobble as one walked through the rib cage-like structure of a serpent.

As they traversed these winding streets, the path inclined uphill, a long and challenging portico that seemed to stretch endlessly. The early sunrise cast patterns of lemon and orange hues through the arches, creating a mesmerising interplay of light that extended beyond the eye's reach. The ascent proved to be a test, both physically and visually, as the ribcage-like arcades guided the traveller towards a destination whose distance remained uncertain.

The local characters of this ascent passed by—the old gentleman with a crooked step, hands clasped behind his back, who walked at an impressive pace. He had been climbing this serpentine route since his youth, his stride unwavering. Meanwhile, the slow traveller, unprepared for the challenge, sighed and heaved with each step as the gentleman effortlessly surpassed them.

Through the tunnel of the portico the traveller's footsteps resonated with the gentle click of the crab's claws and each scuffle of foot on stone with the hiss of the serpent.

The climb, a journey marked by exhaustion and anticipation, unveiled the consecrated ground awaiting at the peak. Perched atop the hill, the centuries-old crab creature sat, its outstretched claws silently beckoning those who sought solace.

The chapter drew to a close as the weary traveller sank onto the nearest bench, their body craving respite. With a deep inhalation, they allowed the tranquillity of the sanctuary to envelop them, their gaze drifting over the arches and alcoves, already planning their next exploration once refreshed.

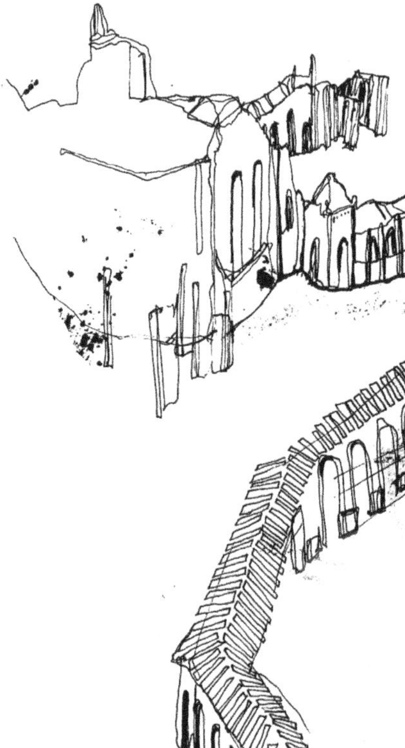

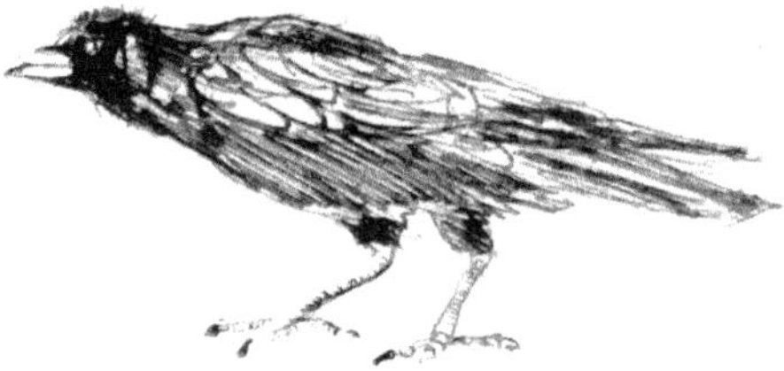

Straying Beyond City Limits

Following the roads outward, into the freshness that passed the peripheral city. Traffic became sparse, the thrum of an engine occasionally passing by. There was still sound of course, the traveller had just opted to swap the constantness of city life to trees, wind and calling birds. It gave the traveller comfort, knowing they weren't alone.

The space the traveller felt was freeing, narrow streets and secretive alleyways were always exciting, intriguing, and held their charm but so did the vastness and details beyond the cityscape. Its appendages sinking into eternal landscapes.

Staying close by the edge of bramble bushes, the traveller arrived at a fork in their path. Sticking out of the wooden signage was an arrow facing east. The inscription written on it however was something the traveller couldn't decipher. The inscription was too faded and worn with age.

Unbothered, the traveller took a chance, taking the route left. This was a day for exploring with no pressing time restraints. Passing livestock in grazed fields, orchards of many kinds, the traveller was taking in the outside world. Yet as time passed, open fields thickened into darkening forests.

Unease twisted in the traveller's stomach as they realised that in search of respite, they had become lost while venturing. Roads turned to lighter, narrower paths. Paths seemed to split into a spiderweb of trails and the traveller was caught in them.

No cellular connection. The wanderer had wandered too far. The traveller was grateful for the trees that offered some shade but a darkening seemed to loom with it.

A caw called from a branch of a birch tree, the traveller turned. Familiar beady eyes met theirs with a head tilted at an observing angle.

"I see you've lost your way, such a shame." The crow preened a feather.

"And yet, you who have found me, I presume, have not," the traveller eyed them back.

"I always know where I am, but landscapes, cityscapes and townscapes change. I have lost places but I am never lost; I will always find places I have been before but knowing for certain if they will remain, I have never known."

The traveller sensed some sorrow from the creature, as if they had mourned more than the traveller had drawn breaths in their time on land.

"So, you are not ever knowing but know what has been. Can you guide me on my way?" They looked up to the crow, whose eyes were now fixed into the distance behind the dense pine trees.

"I do have the knowledge to guide you." The crow did not continue. They had the knowledge. Acquiring it would be a challenge in itself.

"So what will it be? I have no food to offer this time, what about my water?" The traveller swung their bag off their shoulder, beginning to untie its fixtures.

"I am not thirsty nor am I hungry. You may return to me a favour of my choosing," the crow flew a few metres to a previously passed tree, "follow me now. I will be your guide." Quickly, the crow flew, so the traveller hoisted up their backpack, their footsteps becoming a light jog as they trailed the dark wash of flight.

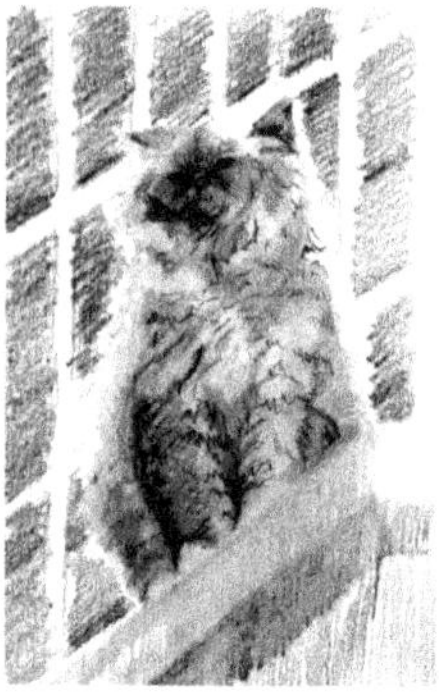

A Summer Day's Tale in the City

Above a quaint flower shop, before the main square, two cats lazily lounged on a white trimmed balcony, basking in the summer sun. The traveller envied these two creatures who had no obligations in life. Simply sun, slumber and supper. Yet they did seem to glare down upon the traveller's paused passing, the ragdoll turning away in dismissal, stretching its fuzzy legs over the windowsill and onto the interior ledge, suggesting a royal indifference.

The other, a shorter haired and rounder in size persian, became animated from his relaxed pose. Their dark body sprang to life, stretching down a pipe as it made its way down the building facade. With a final pounce, their feline instincts landed them carefully on the stone street.

Making confident strides over to the traveller, this cat arched their head and used the traveller's leg as a scratching post. Bending down, the traveller extended a hand, eliciting contented purrs as their fingers traced behind the cat's ears. The idyllic encounter was cut short by the emergence of the flower shop owner, grumbling and reclaiming their feline companion, carrying them back into the shade of the building.

Into the markets the traveller browsed. The square was populated by many stalls and smells. The earthy and slightly fragranced scents of the leather stalls. Roasted hazelnuts by a single vendor enticed their purchase, his quick actions with the flame to ensure timed perfection of roasted nuts was a performance, concluded with the graceful offering of the paper bags. Later, passing sweet pastries watered the mouths and their colours drew eyes. The traveller wished they had two stomachs.

Having found a stone carved seat in the city square, the traveller was due a rested break. Watching crowds pass never bored the traveller, they enjoyed people watching wherever they could. It wasn't until the traveller picked up their belongings to continue their journey that they felt eyes pressing against them. A look around, there was no one in sight. Though, after a moment, a parting in the crowd revealed the dark cat, going as unnoticed as a shadow, peering into the traveller's eyes. The cat, quick to move, pounced across the street where the traveller stood, into the warren of alleyways that formed the city. The traveller wondered if they should follow.

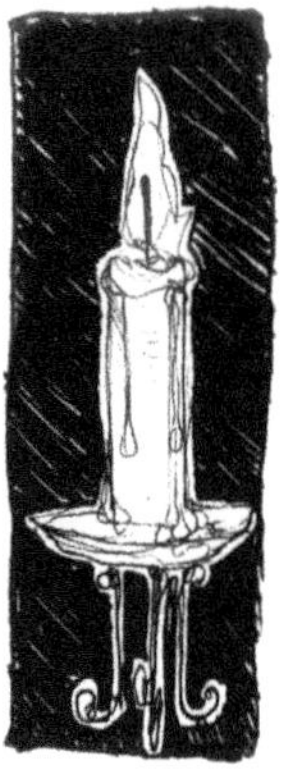

Candles and Oddities: the Charms of Solitude

There happened to be a restaurant that defied the expectations set by its modest exterior. From the outside, it appeared diminutive, a door with a window that doubled its width. However, upon crossing the threshold, the traveller found themself enveloped in elegance and charm.

The ambiance inside was intimate, with dimly lit candles casting a soft glow on silver-plated utensils and embroidered tablecloths. Quirky oddities adorned the walls, while ornate vases and gold-framed pictures adorned the shelves. Seating alone at a table with delicately wired furniture, the traveller marvelled at the aged wooden beams and tiled flooring that extended to the rear, where the restaurant opened up to reveal further seating.

Mirrors strategically hung at angles toward the ceiling, offering obscured views of the dining space below. Intricate floral motifs on golden candelabras added touches of rich warmth to the tables, while shaded lemon walls complemented an oddly placed column, creating the illusion of overlapping structures.

In a corner, an elderly man sat with his back against the wall, absorbed in a device, clear-framed glasses perched low on his nose. The traveller, captivated by the man's contented solitude, couldn't help but occasionally glance in his direction. This establishment, unlike the cafés and bars frequented in moments of solitude, exuded a timeless grandeur unchanged by time, changes in fashion, or the shifting seasons.

As stories were shared and delectable dishes indulged, the setting became a cherished jewel for the traveller to reflect upon—a piece pocketed in memory, where cordiality flowed with each sip of wine. Upon leaving, the elderly man, having sensed the traveller's observant gaze, looked over his rounded glasses and offered a knowing smile, as if acknowledging the silent connection forged through the art of solitude.

A Reread

The solace of literature served well with the sought respite of a warm, spiced beverage at their local establishment. Within their personal effects, a single book occupied a cherished place, its well-worn pages due to countless readings. Accompanying this artefact, a pencil and a collection of adhesive notes served as tools for the traveller's contemplative engagement with the text. Within the margins, carefully underlined passages and expanded annotations revealed a dialogue between reader and author, a silent collaboration unbeknownst to the writer.

This book was like a recurring dialogue. Within each visit emerged new perspectives and contemplations. The dynamic relationship afforded the traveller a unique opportunity for introspection, as they reflected on shared experiences and poignant quotations that resonated with their own narrative. Through the act of annotation, the traveller not only absorbed the tales within the book but also aspired for their own to be as lived and loved as much as the stories in their book were.

With each turn of the page, the traveller rediscovered nuances and details previously missed, much like noticing new facets of the familiar neighbourhood they dwelled in. The act of rereading became a reflective journey through the narrative, offering the traveller fresh insights and perspectives that enriched their understanding of the story, just as revisiting the familiar cityscapes deepened their connection to the urban landscape.

The traveller pulled out their book, an extension of themself and like a diary of sorts. They opened a page in the middle of their book. It was of the sorts where it never mattered which page you opened up on, each chapter was different to the last, they could begin an adventure at any part.

After a few lines of reading the traveller had to reread over the lines of words they found themself unfamiliar with. The traveller definitely wasn't acquitted with this chapter. How after so many times of greeting this book had they missed it?

Perplexed at having found this keyhole of a chapter, the traveller leaning over in excitement at their coffee table, absorbing themself within its pages.

As the traveller delved into the narrative, they found

themself immersed in the story of the man by the window, whose longing gaze extended beyond the café. The man, clad in a black shirt adorned with a lemon motif, sat alone at the bar, embodying a quiet sort of anticipation, his eyes fixed on an empty chair beside him. He had ordered two cups of a steaming hot liquid that fogged the windows by the bar stool he sat at. He took sips consecutively, as if he were counting the times. His hand shook with each. When the minutes accumulated, his drink found itself empty. He placed the cup down to look at the other that remained untouched, cooled from the missing person.

Having looked up from their read, the description in the book mirrored the scene unfolding before the traveller with uncanny precision. The lonely man with two cups, with worry stirring in his eyes as he scanned the outside streets. Head down, the traveller pressed on with their reading.

The tale unfolded like a mystery, a narrative of passion and secrecy. The man was portrayed as part of a couple, his whole self incomplete without his other. They were separated but desperately seeking each other in secrecy. Questions hung in the air like a dense fog: Why were they apart? What drove them to such lengths? Were they fleeing from some unseen danger?

The woman behind the counter frowned at the untouched cup, a silent reproach for the undrunk brew. Oblivious to her disapproval, the man rose from his seat, returning the empty cup and ordering another round. The clink of ceramic against the counter echoed in the café as he persisted, ordering two more cups of hazelnut and cocoa tea. Meanwhile, the man in the traveller's café mirrored these actions, moving in sync with the character on the page. The aroma of freshly brewed tea filled the air, mingling with the scent of anticipation. As the scene unfolded, the traveller found themself immersed in the man's emotions—his worries, his anticipation, his profound love.

Little did he know, his lover would be unable to join him in today's anticipated union, her plans thwarted by unforeseen circumstances. In the narrative, the lovers were meant to reunite in a secret meeting, a moment promising to rekindle their connection. However, fate intervened, leaving the lover unable to reach him.

Desperate to convey her message, she devised a riddle—a code only he would understand. The narrative revealed that the message could only be conveyed by the reader of this chapter, the only one privy to her predicament.

The riddle spoke of a place where lovers whispered secrets sweet, where thorns and fragrance intertwined—a harbour hidden where dreams were born anew. It was a place familiar to them both, a place where their love had blossomed like the flowers that adorned its paths.

As the traveller immersed themself in the narrative

unfolding before them, they couldn't shake the feeling of being drawn into the story, as if they were more than just a passive observer. With each word they read, the emotions of the characters became palpable, their struggles and hopes echoing in the traveller's own heart.

But it wasn't merely curiosity that prompted the traveller to act; it was a profound empathy for the man by the window, whose anticipation and longing mirrored their own. In the pages of the book, they saw reflections of their own desires and fears, and they couldn't bear to witness the man's disappointment without offering a glimmer of hope.

Rising from their seat, the traveller felt a surge of determination, fueled by a sense of duty to bridge the gap between the man and his beloved. It was more than just a chance encounter in a café; it was a moment of connection, a shared experience of longing and yearning for something beyond reach.

As they approached the man, the traveller's heart beat with uncertainty, unsure of how their intervention would be received. They had put the book down by their table. But they knew that they couldn't remain a passive bystander, not when they held the mystery of the riddle.

Getting his attention from the close creaking floorboards and the scrape of a metal stool, the traveller asked if they could sit to speak with the man. He responded that he was due company anytime now, taking another swig of his cup.

The traveller surprised the man with their knowledge, explaining an unforeseen force was at play and they believed they were now a messenger. The traveller pressed on with a hesitant smile, sharing the riddle, watching as recognition dawned on his face.

With gratitude in his eyes, the man offered the traveller a freshly brewed cup of tea, telling of how it was the lover's favourite as a gesture of thanks for bridging the gap between him and his beloved. Together, they sat in companionable silence, the weight of the unspoken message hanging in the air like the fragrance of a rose garden at dusk.

As the man finished his drink and bid farewell to the traveller, expressing his thanks one last time, the traveller accepted the freshly brewed cup with a nod of appreciation. With the warmth of the cup in hand, they returned to their table, their mind still abuzz with the events that had transpired.

Setting the cup down on the table, the traveller reached for their book, intending to resume reading from where they had left off. But as they flipped through the pages, a sense of unease washed over them. Where was the chapter they had been reading? They had forgotten to place their bookmark and now couldn't seem to find the page they were on.

Furrowing their brow in frustration, the traveller

searched through the book, scanning each page in vain. But no matter how many times they flicked through the pages, they couldn't find the chapter about the man and his lover. It was as if the chapter had vanished, leaving behind only a lingering mystery.

With a sigh of resignation, the traveller closed the book, their thoughts still lingering on the unanswered questions. Did the man find his love? What was the resolution to their story? And as they left the café, the warmth of the freshly brewed tea still lingering on their lips, the traveller couldn't help but wonder about the mysterious chapter that had slipped through their fingers, leaving behind only traces of a story partially told.

Supper for One in the Rose Garden

Bathed in the warm glow of summer nights, the traveller found themself in the rose garden. The image of a plump cat, one they had seen captured in a photograph in this very garden, came to mind as they settled into the serene ambiance. With a contented smile, they closed their eyes, mirroring the feline's lazy repose on a wall amid blooming petals.

The hill, steep and comforting, cradled them as they leaned back on elbows. Winding paths of square stones led to different pockets of the garden, where rose bushes from diverse families stood as a living gallery. Summer's embrace was palpable, a prelude to the blossoms soon to retreat behind the city walls.

Seated on the corner of a chequered blanket, their sketchbook lay open, pages secured by pens and pencils against the gentle caress of the light breeze. As the sun descended, painting the skies in hues of pink, amber, and yellow, they reached into their bag.

With a sense of quiet celebration, they retrieved a stemmed glass and a bottle of fizz. Glass raised to the sunset, they cheered to their life, sipping in the sweetness of that moment and the many more to come.

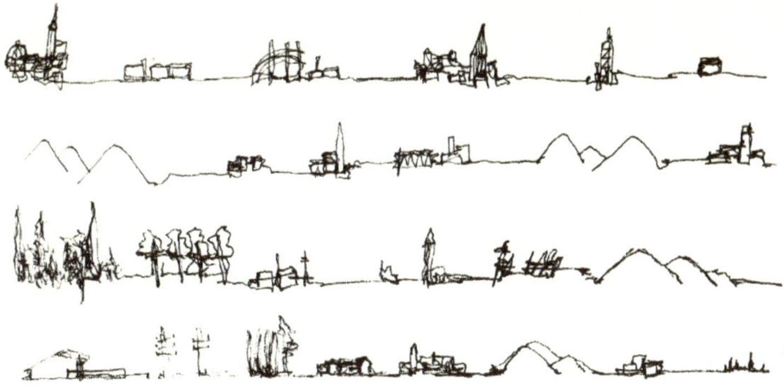

Moments of Centralisation and Abandonment, and Places in Between

Embarking on their journey, heed the wisdom: start early and venture far, for the day promised to be long and wearisome for the traveller. The relentless sun beating down, leaving the skin irritated, and a persistent thirst gripping at the traveller's throat, though water remained elusive, they must be sparring. Yet, in this harshness, they found comfort in a companion who shared this arduous expedition.

Heading westward as sunlight painted the sky in a burst of amber, their travels demanded a mosaic of transportation methods. The yearning for the ocean's tranquil feeling pulling them forward, a balm to soothe the weariness borne from recent busyness and clamour. Along the way, they passed through villages with houses adorned in sun-drenched yellows and faded reds. Some of these

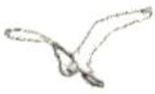

dwellings were even to be spotted in the expanse of what some would dain nowhere. Noticing true solitude was always a rarity.

Their path led them past fading structures and derelict buildings, their crumbling façades whispered stories of times long gone. They almost felt the chalky residue clinging to their fingers if they were to reach out and touch them. In the mind's eye, they envisioned climbing these skeletal remains, their forms resilient yet fragile, hoping they would bear the weight enough to reach its summit. They imagined hands on the zig-zagged bars, sensing their warmth and even catching a whiff of the metallic scent that left a chill settling in their mouth.

Amidst this urban decay, a pattern emerged: moments of centralization, fleeting and few, followed by the sprawl of suburbs, and then a brief respite before larger, more imposing structures loom into view. Some stand tall and alive, teeming with purpose, while others lie in abandonment, their life force drained by neglect.

The journey became a log of landscapes, cityscapes and townscapes. A continuous line drawing of forms, eyes running over horizons, capturing their outlines.

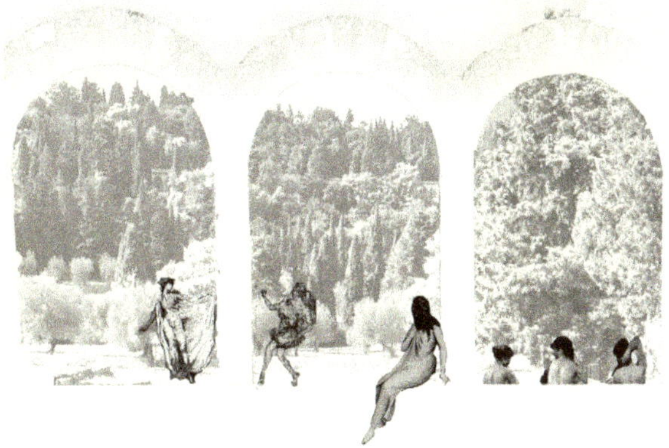

Three Arches, Three Tales

In this city, where ancient ruins transcended the boundaries of time, the traveller came upon three arches. Each arch whispered stories of nymphs, maidens, and tranquil gatherings. Through the traveller's gaze, these narratives converged, creating a multidimensional viewing that captured essences of bygone eras.

Within the first arch, nymphs materialised, ethereal beings whose joyous dance transformed the stone structure into a timeless stage. Their ceaseless energy, a boundless craze of spiralling figures of eight, weaved through the ancient stones. Laughter, both enchanting and relentless, echoed as they playfully anchored themselves on sturdy columns. Their delicate hands, adorned with freshly picked flowers entangled in their hair, brushed against the weathered stone, leaving a trace of their spirited play. The enticing scent of the flowers permeated the air, creating an alluring atmosphere that drew the traveller in.

In this ethereal dance, the nymphs' bare feet skipped on the warm stone, adding a rhythmic percussion that intensified the sensory symphony. The billowing fabric of their white attire swayed with each spirited movement, creating a mesmerising display. As the nymphs invited the traveller to join their playful steps, a subtle worry crept in – a concern that the human spirit may struggle to match the boundless energy of these ethereal beings, caught in a craze that knows no bounds. The invitation to dance became both enchanting and daunting, blurring the lines between reality and the timeless realm of the nymphs.

Transitioning to the second arch, a maiden with resplendent tresses reclined gracefully at the edge, her legs suspended above the halcyon waters. Bathed in the gentle caress of sunlight, she savoured a moment of introspection, occasionally submerging her toes, conjuring undulating ripples across the placid surface. Her gaze beheld the natural scene beyond, where clusters of trees ascended the verdant hill, touched by sunlight and shadow.

This ingénue, delicately poised on the precipice of womanhood, felt the weight of her musings intensify. Peering towards the hill, she envisioned the weathered trees scaling the summit. Each tree, weathering the passage of time, became a metaphor for her own life journey. Would she seamlessly integrate into the intricate fabric of time, like the trees merging into one another, or would she emerge distinct, soaring above the collective? The landscape begot profound queries, enduring in their relevance. Nestled against the comforting warmth of the stone, her back cradled, eyes sealed in introspection, she began to weave dreams of the life she yearned to unfold. This tableau painted a poignant portrait of a spirit navigating the intricacies of existence, caught between the purity of youth and the enigmatic realms of maturity.

Within the final arch, obscured heads and partially submerged bodies formed a picturesque montage of tranquil repose. A symphony of muted conversations blended with the gentle lap of water caressing stone boundaries. Faces tilted towards the sun, bathing in its heat on their skin, while a delicate breeze imparted a subtle coolness to the idyllic scene. Amid the vestiges of ancient ruins, this assemblage of individuals discovered solace, their collective serenity standing in stark contrast to the lively tales etched into the arches.

Darkened strands of hair, drenched in water, clung tenaciously to skin, adorned with droplets that shimmered briefly before yielding to the midday sun's caress. Whispers traversed the water's surface, murmurs that wove into a background hum, scarcely registering. The ebb and flow of attendees, some departing and others arriving, orchestrated a subtle rhythm, akin to the muted ambiance of a library. Departures resonated louder, while arrivals cloaked themself in hushed quietude. Here, conversations materialised as subtle rustlings, mirroring the hallowed silence of a sanctum sanctorum, underscoring the notion that tranquillity is a shared treasure in this aqueous haven.

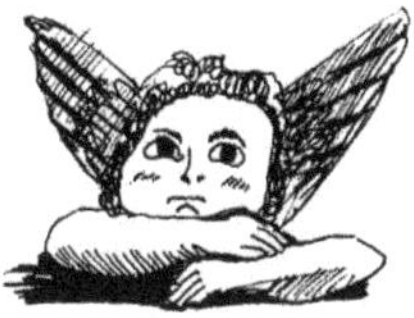

FOTOAUTOMATICA

The photobooth, a charming relic nestled at the crossroads of the city, beckoned the traveller and their companion with its classic red facade. A whimsical baby cupid adorned the booth, perched atop the yellow end street, seemingly watching over the photographic proceedings.

Eager for a tactile memento of their journey, the duo joined a small queue, the allure of an adjacent ice cream shop already promising a delightful follow-up. Taking their place on the singular seat in front of the camera, they squeezed in, ready to capture a snapshot of their shared adventure.

The clinking sound of a coin dropping into the slot initiated the process, and the first flash bathed them in paper-white light. The subsequent moments involved a ballet of tilted heads, meeting eyes, and playful gestures—

efforts to freeze their camaraderie in time. The anticipation built as they awaited the four photos to emerge on the strip, a slow reveal in contrast to the instant gratification of modern photography.

There was a certain intrinsic quality in possessing a physical copy of their memories right there on the spot. The wait, the uncertainty of the outcome, and the hum of the developing process all added to the charm. As the images materialised, a sense of joy and nostalgia filled the air. The final product, a tangible strip of memories, became an invaluable treasure—a piece of paper carrying the essence of their shared journey. Tearing the strip in half, each holding a portion, they now possessed a reminder of their unique bond and the adventures captured in those four frames.

The Heron of the City's Waterways

In the serene shelter of the city, tucked along the leisurely meanders of the river, a heron reigned supreme, its elegant figure perched proudly at the core of the weir. Its stance, regal and unwavering, echoed the commanding presence of the statues gracing the city's refined squares. The distant horizon of the river heated with hues of a blazing sunset, casting a fiery palette across the water, while the heron, an embodiment of poise and majesty, emerged as a striking silhouette against the vibrant evening sky. Here, in the natural grandeur, it was a living sculpture.

But the heron, in its daily rituals of stalking and standing, was oblivious to the spectacle it unwittingly crafted. Following the meandering path of the water, it glided gracefully along the riverbank, surpassing even the most skilled rowers. In the daylight hours, its presence was conspicuous, a feature that stood out against the idyllic surroundings, easily catching the observer's eye. Yet, as night descended, the heron became a phantom, elusive and mysterious, hidden within the obsidian depths, although its essence lingered, a reminder of its perpetual presence.

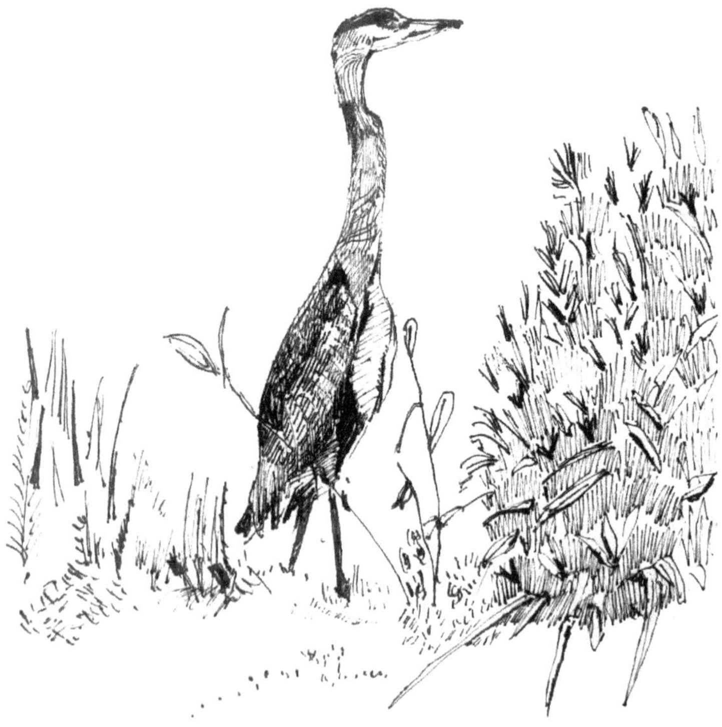

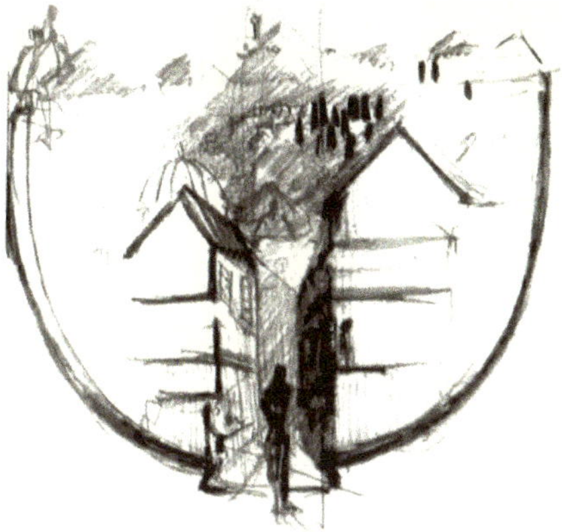

Hills and Structures in Harmonious Play

On the side of the bowl, the traveller's eyes traced the gentle dips and edges, mapping the contours of its form. The traveller observed the rolling hills of the bowl's interior playfully undulating, their peaks and troughs overlapping in a lively interplay. Occasionally, where the slopes met architectural structures, there was a subtle nod, a silent greeting exchanged.

In the centre of the bowl, only fragments of these edges were visible as the dish revolved around them, creating a shifting panorama of perspectives and dimensions. The scene resembled the stage set of a pantomime, essential for the story of the play, but the focus remained on the actors – in this case, the architectural forms that shaped the cityscape. Perched on the rim, their eyes roamed, taking in the bejeweling landscape of these hills, each curve and incline an enjoyable coaster for the eye.

From the very centre of this bowl, these sights took on a different angle. They revealed themselves only when the streets, like guiding pathways, directed the traveller's gaze down their lengthy stretches. In those moments, the detailed interplay of slopes and structures became apparent, crafting a variety of visual wonders as the traveller traversed the city.

Yet, the full appreciation of this pantomime set revealed itself only when the traveller found themself on the edge of the city, high above, where the hills completed a loop. From this vantage point, the ensemble of structures, hills, and winding streets formed a considerable masterpiece. The completed loop of hills accentuated the carefully crafted design, making the traveller realise that the beauty of the pantomime set, much like the city itself, was best comprehended when one understood both inside and outside the centre, standing on the rim, and feeling the pulse of life in the heart of this broth. Much like a customer who, when the dish is served, sees the masterpiece and savours its composition, architectural nuances and intricate flavours.

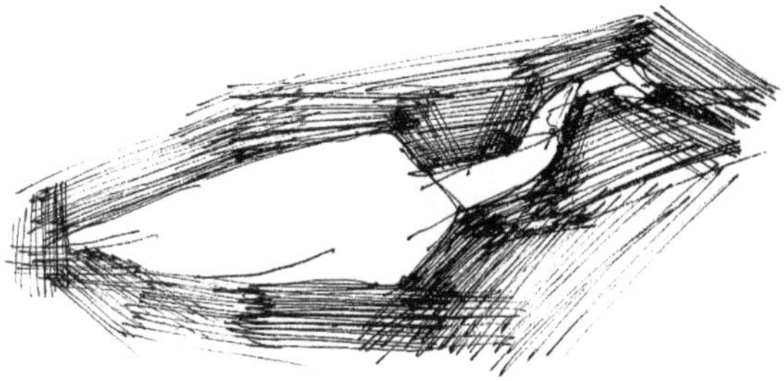

Elegance in Stillness

Unfurling, like a delicate petal, the egret, standing gracefully on the weir, reminded the traveller of the times when their mother brought home lilies. The traveller would always find themself gazing out of their kitchen window, but when these lilies were placed on the windowsill, there was only a certain amount of time for appreciation before they withered. A tall, thin, glass vase, carefully chosen, would centre the blooms against the wide window. Mornings were spent tracing their delicate forms. Bright light streamed into the room, interacting with the translucent petals, casting delicate shadows and illuminating their intricate veins. It seemed as if the light was there solely for the lilies, enhancing their fleeting beauty. Both egret and lily possessed that striking presence, a delicate beauty that would always captivate the traveller's gaze.

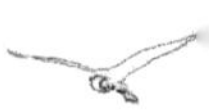

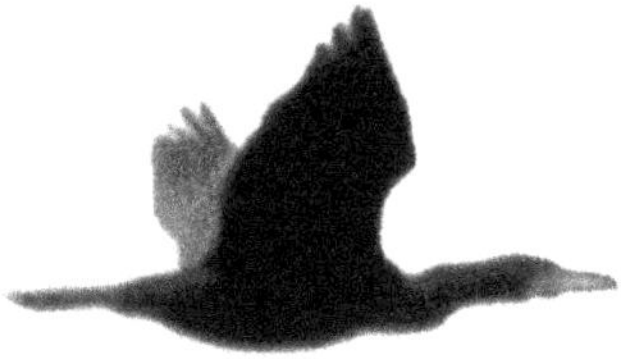

From Riffle to Skyline

Perched on a rock by the riffle, before the run, the cormorant preened its feathered breast with the sharp, hooked end of its beak. Its sleek, black plumage glistened in the sunlight as the bird tended to its waterproof feathers, readying itself for another underwater hunting expedition.

Later in the day this bird was to be observed by the traveller only in passing flight. Upon the third bridge east, the traveller spotted the cormorant, a living black arrow shooting at a low, far range from the base of another bridge to the pinnacle of the one on which the traveller stood. The cormorant's swift and purposeful flight was a captivating visual of a black, arching, serpentine shadow as it soared across playful façades.

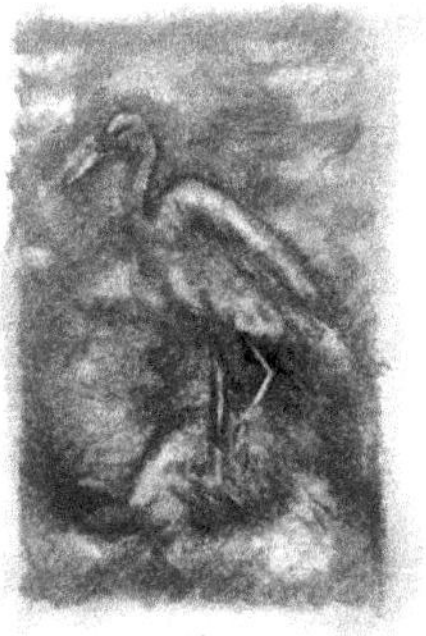

Patrol Beneath the Bridge

As the traveller ambled along the elevated path, high above the meandering river, they paused to immerse themself in the richness of life unfolding below. Conversations flowed like the gentle current, people strolling by, engaged in animated dialogue. A balcony adorned with individuals sipping wine became a fleeting vignette, while a nearby bench hosted a scene of leisure, where ice cream was enjoyed with shared laughter from quickly melting dessert. In the distance, the rhythmic clip-clop of horses could be heard disappearing into the crowds.

The traveller's eyes panned from the liveliness of the streets to a different sort at the river. Peering down, their eyes locked on a creature concentrating on movements through the water.

In the haunt beneath the bridge, the egret commanded

his territory with a demeanour reminiscent of a fairy tale troll, patiently awaiting the passage of unsuspecting souls. Yet, this majestic creature took on the duty of a vigilant knight, patrolling to either side of the bridge and back, a silent watcher in the shadows.

With each stride, his forked, clawed feet cut through the water like sticks of black licorice, leaving only the slightest ripples in his wake. The speared beak, poised and ready, pulled back in anticipation of a viper-quick attack. His movements were swift and nimble, a fluid blade slicing through the water with precision. The egret, a scout beneath the bridge, embodied both the enchantment of folklore and the grace of a warrior as it struck and caught prey.

Evening Sonata

As the night draped itself over the city, the traveller found themself on a balcony overlooking the river below, accompanied by a newfound companion. Their friendship had blossomed from chance encounters and shared tales, experiences and whispered confidences.

Seated side by side, they exchanged stories of adventures both current and past, laughter mingling with the murmur of the river's song. The traveller regaled their companion with anecdotes of busy markets, winding streets, and chance encounters with colourful characters along their journey.

But as the conversation flowed, the companion's gaze lingered on the waters below, an overlooked observer amidst the cityscape. With a thoughtful expression, they remarked upon the significance of the river, how it anchored the stories of the city, its banks harbouring life and history.

"It's curious," the companion mused, turning to the traveller, "you've shared tales of those who walk by the river, of the activities that unfold along its banks, but you've yet to speak of the river itself. What stories does it hold, I wonder?"

The traveller paused, struck by the companion's observation. In all their adventures and storytelling, they had passed over the line that split the city, its currents carrying untold tales and secrets within its depths. With a smile, the traveller accepted the challenge, their mind already spinning with the promise of new narratives waiting to be discovered along the river's edge.

"Fellow companion," the response came, the voice laden with a sense of contemplation, "you're right; the river, in all its quiet majesty, often remains unspoken in the tales of the city. It's a constant companion to every story the city holds. It flows, timeless and eternal, witnessing life and death along its banks."

The traveller's tone softened, the words flowing like the very river they spoke of, "Sometimes the life of busyness does threaten to overshadow the natural poetry of the river. Yet, how could I forget? The river is more than just water, it's a mirror to the city's soul.

"On a late night, after the world had quieted down, I walked along its banks. It was almost too dark to see until the flick of a light switch illuminated the surroundings. The river mirrored this transformation and became an actor in this nightly play. First, a crescendo – covered in confetti-like lights, the river shimmered like a woman adorned in gold on a festive night. As she moved, the wind breathed over her, sending ripples across her surface, catching twinkles of what adorned her. It was a dance with the night, a ballet of shadows and glimmers, and in those moments, the river became more than a mere watercourse – it became a living entity that reflected the current of time."

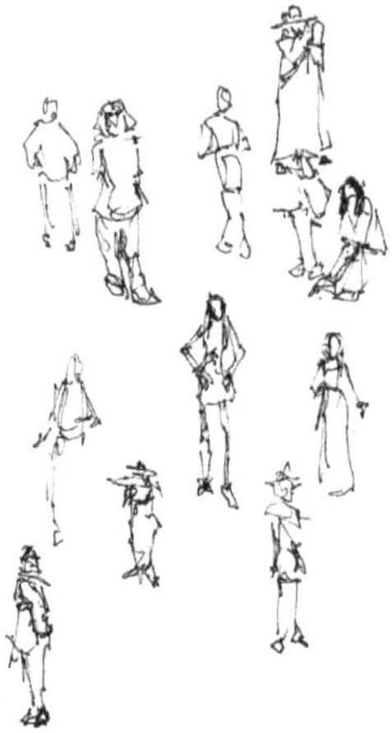

Sunday Streets

On a Sunday morning, the city came alive with the unveiling of a master's art collection, drawing crowds into queues that snaked through streets and alleys. Amid this creation of anticipation, the traveller strolled leisurely, attuned to the collective curiosity that hung in the air.

In an apartment above, a woman stirred from her Sunday residence, intrigued by distant murmurs disturbing the morning calm. Barefoot, she approached the window, unveiling a street tableau. Her gaze widened at the sight of a mysterious queue weaving through her city's streets, its purpose obscured. At the tail end, where its destination remained elusive, her curiosity deepened.

As the queue meandered outside her building, the woman became an unseen spectator to the arrival of the solitary traveller. With quiet confidence, the traveller seamlessly joined a group near a corner coffee shop, orchestrating breakfast runs and laughter. The camaraderie unfolded, drawing the woman's gaze with its subtle complexities.

While the traveller engaged with the group, the woman found herself captivated by the unfolding narratives—eloquent introductions, shared smiles, and the exchange of stories. The aroma of coffee wafted up, carrying warmth and connection that excelled the physical distance.

In a serendipitous moment, the traveller's eyes met hers from below, a fleeting connection that bridged the gap between their worlds. For a brief instant, the woman at the window felt part of the lively happening through the Sunday morning streets. Unbeknownst to her, the day held surprises and shared stories, painting the city with hues of unexpected connections.

Performances of Poses and Preening by Peculiar Pigeons

During what could be considered the traveller's typical daily routine, they passed through the park located on the edge of town on their way into the city centre. More often than not, the traveller passed on their lunch break, despite its lack of lushness it possessed a peculiar charm. The ground was covered in wood chips and dirt and shaded by ancient trees that created a dappled pattern of light and shadow. However, it was at noon when the sun pierced through the canopy, illuminating a modest fountain that became the centre of avian activity.

This fountain, though relatively small, was a hub of energy, especially for a peculiar community of pigeons. Unlike their counterparts in other destinations, these pigeons were of a smaller size, yet they exuded a vibrant charisma. At the stroke of noon, they descended upon the fountain, their presence turning it into a lively spectacle. Queueing was a foreign concept to these pigeons; instead, they employed a jump and a flap, accompanied by assertive "make way for me" gestures as they carved out spaces for themselves. In their eccentric tango, wings spread wide, sprinkling specks of water, posing and preening under the radiant midday sun.

Strangely, the traveller hadn't paid much attention to the fountain's statue until a day when their timing was off, and the pigeons had already departed. It was then they noticed four brass boys, each with a cherubic cupid's face, stacked one upon the other, mirroring the pose of the next. They were on hands and knees, forming a tower, with a tortoise, a recurring motif in the city, bearing their weight beneath. The traveller found it intriguing, realising that weeks had passed before they had ever truly seen this charming and whimsical structure, hidden beneath the lively performances of the pigeons.

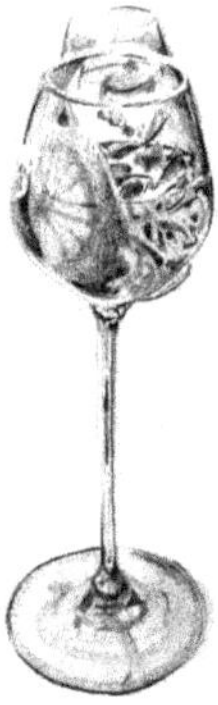

Notes of Kinship: An Evening Unfolds at the Café

The traveller had found their usual spot at the café, a corner where familiarity wrapped around them like a comforting shroud. The café workers recognised their face, and with every visit, the traveller picked up the nuances of the language, weaving themself deeper into the fabric of the place.

On this particular evening, the hours had stretched from late afternoon into night, as time always seemed to stretch when shared with a companion. This kindred spirit, akin to the traveller in essence, exchanged tales filled with familiarities and recurring themes. Laughter skipped across the table of drinks, embracing the night like an old friend. The clinking of plates and glasses signalled that it was time to return them to the service. In the midst of conversation, the day's academic discussions effortlessly melted into personal stories, a bridge crossed from mere companionship to friendship.

The atmosphere of the café shifted subtly as locals trickled in, infusing the space with an unspoken sense of belonging. The staff, who were already friendly, became even more so, leaving their posts behind the bar to exchange kisses and warm greetings with the patrons. Seated by a window, the traveller noticed a piano, previously overlooked, now standing in all its grandeur. It had appeared as a mere cabinet or shelf, adorned with glass lamps that cast a soft glow on the crimson wall, which itself was plastered with an assortment of unusual photographs depicting figures with octopuses.

Warmth filled the air as the pianist, their fingers delicately pressing the keys, coaxed rich and joyous melodies from the instrument. The music hung in the air, captivating the ears of everyone present, drawing spontaneous applause after the informal first set. Encouraged by the friends' warm smiles, the pianist continued their performance. The evening wore on, the friends staying longer than planned, enchanted by the music and the atmosphere. Eventually, they found themself laughing with the bar staff, exchanging playful banter as they mimicked the staff's choice of limoncello, their shared camaraderie intertwining yet another element into the collage of the night.

Tales of the River and City

Upon the banks, the river ran with a purpose known to few. In a short distance, the traveller spotted a stick, weathered and worn, lying idle on the riverbank. With a flick of the wrist, the traveller picked up the stick and tossed it into the river. Their eyes followed its journey as it was carried by the current, weaving in and out of eddies and riffles.

This river stretched far beyond the view of the eye. The traveller was stationed by a southward curve, tracing its path from the mountains before it meandered far to meet the western coast.

As day bled into night, sun bled into the river. World ending colours cast upon the proceeding water. The traveller pondered the river's untold stories, tales of cunning tactics, of a liquid weapon wielded with hydraulic mastery. A city, a place of art and intrigue, once turned this serene waterway into a strategic ally.

In times of conflict, the power of the river was harnessed, diverting its waters with calculated precision. The flow became a weapon, flooding the territories of rival cities, thanks to the ingenuity and tactical prowess of engineering. As the traveller stood by the river, their eyes fixated on the stick, its journey seeming rather insignificant.

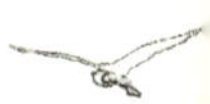

A Culinary Interlude

Embarking on a tale of taste, the narrative unfurled with the anticipation of a well-deserved lunch break. Within the commotion and activity of the midday rush, the traveller navigated the paths to the eatery with practised ease. Lucky in their foresight, they had already decided on their order, ensuring a swift selection amidst the cacophony of kitchen utensils and animated conversations.

Vibrant arrays of assorted meats beckoned from behind glass displays, each slice meticulously prepared by diligent workers who moved with purpose and determination. Every individual worker played their part with unwavering commitment.

Customers spilled in and out like streams of consciousness, their exchanges swift and efficient. Cash changed hands in a seamless transaction, and before long, each patron emerged victorious, clutching a prized packet.

Venturing out into the nearby square, the traveller found themself among a congregation of fellow diners, benches filled to capacity. Undeterred, they settled for the base of a lamppost, an impromptu dining spot in the beat of the midday sun. Nearby sparrows, ever vigilant for crumbs, circled eagerly, their presence adding a touch of whimsy to the scene.

With anticipation palpable in the air, the traveller unwrapped their parcel, the distinctive red and white paper yielding to reveal the coveted treasure within. The aroma wafted up, a prelude to the feast that awaited. Without hesitation, the traveller took their first bite, savouring the textures and flavours upon their palate. A crisp crunch gave way to a soft, pillowy interior, each mouthful a revelation of culinary craftsmanship.

In the midst of their enjoyment, the traveller spared a thought for their avian companions, knowing full well that there would be little left for them to scavenge. But in that moment, in the shared delight of the meal, there was a sense of unity—a reminder that even in the most mundane of activities, there was magic to be found.

A Melodic Journey Along the River

As the traveller and their new companion strolled along the riverbanks, the path took an unexpected turn, leading them away from the busyness of the city. The river they followed seemed like a quieter sibling to the main watercourse, and the hectic city slowly faded into the background.

Amidst the reposeful waterway, previously known to the traveller as a thin, blue line forking from the central river on maps, the traveller's senses worked to hear a faint melody under the tune of the waterflow. It was as if a chorus of voices whispered in harmony from the past. Entranced by the song, the traveller and their friend decided to follow the enchanting tune, drawing closer to the river's edge.

As they approached, the sound of water trickling over

rocks and pebbles intermingled with the distant echoes of a women's song. The voices seemingly young yet old, carrying with them the echoes of days long gone. The traveller felt as if they were eavesdropping on a scene from the past, where women gathered by the riverbank to wash clothes, their voices weaving a togetherness of song. They sang of their gatherings and current tasks at the river as they scrubbed, rinsed, and dried clothes, taking advantage of the flowing water.

The melody persisted, an ageless song that capered along the riverbank of the enduring stories etched into the landscapes of rivers and the lives they touched.

Whispers in Brass

As the traveller wandered through the city's neighbourhoods, they were drawn to the distinctive door handles that adorned many homes. Positioned at eye level, these entryway fixtures, often accessible via a few steps, consistently caught the traveller's attention.

These door handles became an integral part of the streetscape, enhancing the city's rich architectural character. Whether walking briskly or standing still, the traveller found solace in these details. They provided a point of focus, a way to pass time, each one unique in design yet unified in its presence.

A particular window gleamed with a brass allure, catching the traveller's eye. Upon closer inspection, it revealed a collection of individual handles and knockers—an archive of cast faces, each silently awaiting acknowledgment.

Their eyes hopped from one corner of the window to the next, attempting to absorb the varied treasure trove. Realising the countless variations, they paused their excitement, examining each piece as if searching for a specific book in a library.

Amidst the accumulation confined within the small shop window, the traveller lifted their gaze, hoping to spot more light-fractured faces beyond the glass.

Each handle whispered a unique narrative, a tale of those who had crossed the threshold. Momentarily lost in contemplation, the traveller felt a deep appreciation for the city's silent storytellers.

With a final, lingering glance, the traveller reluctantly continued their journey, knowing that these door handles would remain etched in their memory—a collection of personal touches that, like the city itself, invited exploration and discovery at every turn.

To be a River

To be a river, fluent in the language of motion, its banks aged and serene, a peripheral between the fuss of the city. Downstream, where water caresses stone with tender care, one must tread cautiously, lest a misstep leads to despair. Does the river chase the city's constancy, or is it the reverse? Perhaps two facets of one truth. A present salve, it soothes with ripples and riffs. Not forgotten, but often overlooked from bridges and banks. Reflecting stories day and night from the bird spotted with their catch to the balcony that hosts late-night sips of wine. The pathway for rowers and a runway for avian flight, and a respite from narrow streets. In the hush of night, it stirs, kissed by a thousand stars. Reflecting streetlamps like golden evening cigars and the moon's gentle glow. An animated presence found in the city's nocturnal scene. To exist as a river is to embody life from day and night. Guardian of a city's ancient secrets. To exist as a river is to be an everlasting entity, embraced by the city's fond caress.

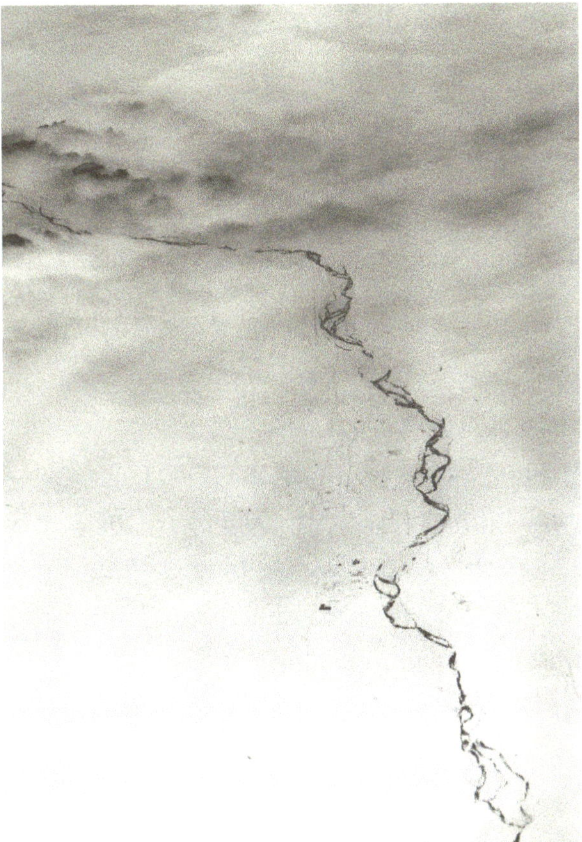

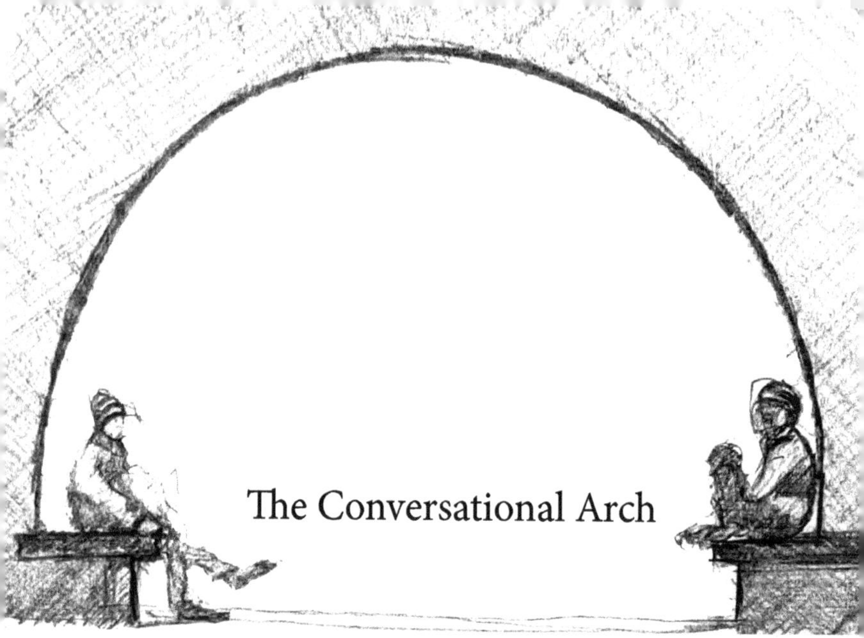

The Conversational Arch

Under the eternal arches, where history whispered in every stone, two figures found their seats at the arch's base points. It was the happening of an opus. Their conversation, with lilt, resonated through the air, amplified by the arch's acoustics. These men, engaged in mirrored gestures, were unwitting actors on a stage crafted by the arch's grandeur. Each word reverberated within the stone embrace, lending an aura of profundity to their dialogue. The arch transformed into a metaphorical microphone, capturing the nuances of their discourse, infusing the space with energy and the allure of conversation.

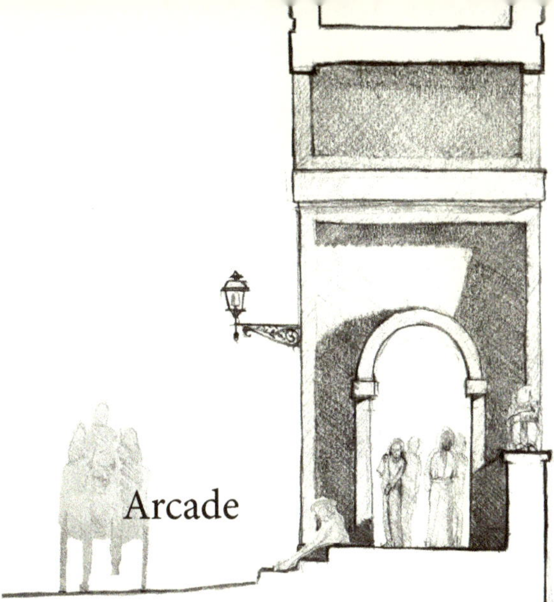

Arcade

En route from the east, toward their destination, a spectacle lined before the traveller. These arches, eloquent in their continuity, guided the traveller through a corridor of frames. Each step beneath their majestic sweep revealed vistas of the river and the cityscape beyond. Bathed in the moments of sunlight filtering through, these arches offered poetry of light and shadow. In between each frame, where those peering over riverbank walls. They caught respite before joining back in with the quick paced flow of the passageway the arches provided.

Hitchhiker

A content wee creature accompanied the traveller today, backpacking along. The traveller's shoulder served as a landing pad for its tired wings to recover. Eyes, legs, and body all green, the creature almost resembled a leaf.

"All is well, my little friend," the traveller thought aloud. "See that point beyond the river, where the trees part and the hills meet? That's our route today."

It was unexpected, this companionship. The traveller hadn't sought it, but they believed it would suit both of them well. The creature seemed weary, while the traveller was full of energy. Light as a feather, the creature needed to watch out for the wind—it might catch it. The traveller urged it to hold tight and enjoy the day's sights together..

A Day of Unexpected Bookstore Encounters

Upon noticing something once, it happens often to encounter it again on the same day. The traveller found themself pondering this phenomenon after stumbling upon several bookstores and libraries in a single morning. Although the idea of visiting one had been lingering in their mind, they had not actively sought them out.

The first bookstore beckoned the traveller with a gentle melody emanating from within. A young man, seated at the back of the store, was immersed in playing the piano, his features obscured by a shaggy curtain of hair. Yet, his music revealed the essence of the store to the traveller, inviting them inside.

Only moments away stood another bookstore, and then another. It struck the traveller as peculiar how these establishments seemed to unveil themself one after the other, as if serenading them to step inside. One of these stores lay hidden in the basement of a main street, its presence masked by the unassuming entrance. Witnessing a couple emerge, their heads bobbing as they ascended from the underground, piqued the traveller's curiosity. With time to spare and no pressing engagements, they descended the weathered wooden steps, mindful not to stumble.

Inside, the store defied expectations with its surprisingly bright ambiance. Floor-to-ceiling shelves overflowed with books, illuminated by an unseen source, dispelling the darkness that enveloped the basement. An elderly man, clad in a knitted cream and green vest, occupied a hunched position behind the counter, a comforting presence between the chill seeping in from the street outside.

The traveller was drawn to the aged figure behind the counter, whose weathered face seemed to echo the well-worn pages of the books surrounding them. The old man's eyes gleamed with a depth of knowledge, the traveller felt an immediate sense of intrigue. Engaging in conversation, the traveller discovered that the old man has spent a lifetime immersed in the world of literature, curating the store's collection with a meticulous care born of passion and reverence. His stories illustrated a life lived in pursuit of knowledge and understanding.

They felt as though they were in the presence of a living library, each line etched into his weathered skin a chapter of his storied life. Despite his age, there was a vitality to his words, a timeless quality that spoke to storytelling. The wisdom and stories from the old man was a gift in itself.

Leaving the store, in that brief encounter, they glimpsed the depths of human experience, finding solace in the knowledge that even in the vast expanse of the world, there are still pockets of wisdom waiting to be discovered.

Thoughts on Cafés, Bookstores and Libraries

The traveller, with their trusty travel book in hand, wandered the city, reflecting on the places they had found solace in reading.

In the hallowed halls of libraries, the air was filled with whispered words and rustling pages. Here, the primary purpose was the celebration of knowledge and the written word. Rows upon rows of shelves stood stacked with text, each one a treasure waiting to be uncovered. Libraries were often marked by a solemn ambiance, with individuals engrossed in the world of literature, studying, or researching. There might have been reading nooks, but conversations were held in muted tones, acknowledging the collective reverence for reading.

Bookstores, on the other hand, were gateways to exploration and discovery. While they shared the love for books with libraries, there was a different energy. Visitors were encouraged not just to peruse the shelves but to actively engage with the books, flipping through pages, and perhaps enjoying a cup of coffee. Bookstores often had a curated selection, sometimes reflecting the personality and interests of the owner. Conversations and laughter were more welcome here, creating an atmosphere of shared enthusiasm for literature.

Cafés were the cosy corners where the aroma of coffee mingled with the scent of freshly baked pastries. While not dedicated to books, many cafes understood the allure of pairing a good read with a cup of coffee. Some might have even offered a selection of books for patrons to enjoy during their visit. Conversations flowed freely, and the ambiance was more dynamic, making it an inviting space for both solitary reading and social gatherings.

In this literary landscape, the lines between these havens of wordsmithery often blurred. Libraries might have housed cafés and bookstores, offering a multifaceted experience. Bookstores might have invited readers to linger in cosy corners with a cup of coffee, blurring the lines between commerce and contemplation. Cafés might have sold books, becoming a haven for literary enthusiasts seeking both caffeine and stories.

Whether one sought the profound silence of a library, the interactive buzz of a bookstore, or the laid-back charm of a cafe, each space catered to a different facet of the reading and social experience.

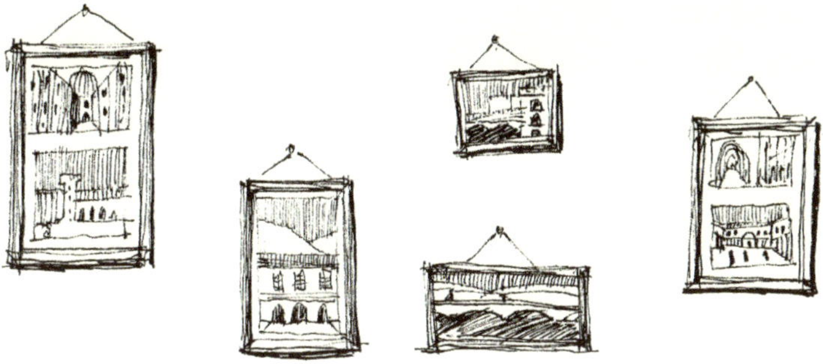

Echoes of Cityscapes

Around the hearth of the traveller's abode, a gallery of framed drawings adorned the walls, each telling stories of bygone eras. The frames, rebelliously hung at varying heights, invited the eyes to spring across the room in waves, creating a warm and inviting atmosphere. It was a curated chaos, a deliberate departure from the strict lines of conventional galleries.

Each drawing held a piece of history, a frozen moment in the evolution of cityscapes. Towers teetered and vistas stretched, capturing the essence of places transformed by the wear of time. In these visual narratives, horses pulled wagons, and skirts cascaded in layers, brushing against the dusty floors of a bygone world. The traveller played a mental game of spot-the-difference, comparing the scenes of hectic squares, where the definition of 'busy' had shifted across the ages.

The architectural grandeur stood prominently in each drawing, highlighting the centrality of these structures in the life of the depicted city. However, the traveller, having stood amidst those very scenes, knew that the grandeur and greatness could never be fully captured within the confines of a picture. In the drawings, squares teemed with activities, yet the traveller realised that what seemed less crowded in the older depictions would have been considered a lively spectacle in its time.

In one such square that the traveller had visited, a carousel gleamed like a beacon for all ages, surrounded by a jazz group of impeccably dressed older men. A comparison observing the drawing seemed frozen in time, oblivious to the passing cars that now frequented the once pedestrianised space. The traveller's mind wandered through the images, conjuring moments of live action that briefly came alive before returning to stillness.

As the traveller immersed themself in the stories these drawings whispered, a realisation dawned. An image, frozen in time, might tell a story, but it was a story frozen in someone else's narrative. Perhaps, the traveller mused, they had no right to impose their interpretation on these scenes, for these drawings were remnants of someone else's journey, someone else's story captured in still frames.

The long layered skirts on dusty floors told tales of a different rhythm, a pace set by the shuffle of footsteps in an era long past. And as the traveller continued to gaze, they noticed the absence of vibrant city sounds in these images, a silence broken only by the hushed murmurs of distant voices and the rustle of long skirts.

In the drawings, the architecture stood bold in isolation, framed against the backdrop of a quieter time. The traveller observed how these structures, so prominently showcased in the images, would now be lost in a sea of people if visited in the present moment. The reality was that the grandeur captured in the drawings was hidden behind the constant movement of modern life.

To truly appreciate the architectural beauty without the intrusion of crowds, the traveller mused, one would need to wander the city's streets in the late evening when stores had closed their shutters. It was during those quiet hours, preceding the morning songbirds, that the essence of the depicted scenes could be glimpsed without the masses, allowing the traveller to connect with the architectural soul of the city.

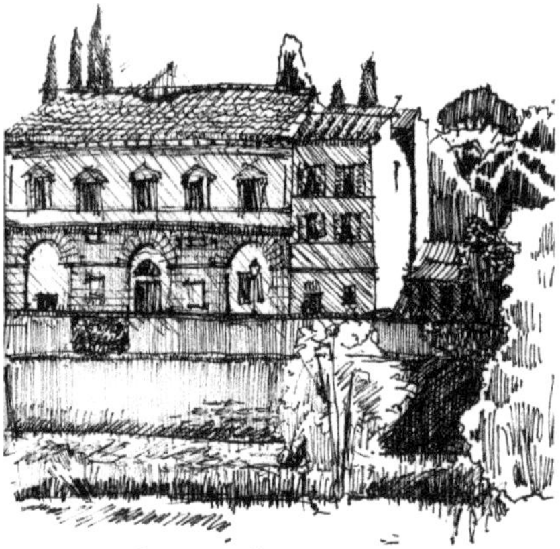

Interplay of City and River

As the city's rhythm approached the river's edge, buildings, with their stoic facades and intricate designs, leaned boldly over the water, their reflections dancing on the rippling surface below. On the northern side, the atmosphere adopted a warmer tone. In the daylight hours, locals leisurely occupied the riverbank wall, savouring sandwiches, basking in the sun, and capturing the picturesque bridges and water with their cameras.

On the opposite shore, restaurants stretched daringly over the water, transforming the river into a bustling thoroughfare reminiscent of a waterborne highway. It was a dynamic interplay of urban and aquatic realms. A mere five-minute stroll in either direction revealed a panorama of perpetual movement, where the city and the river seamlessly coalesced.

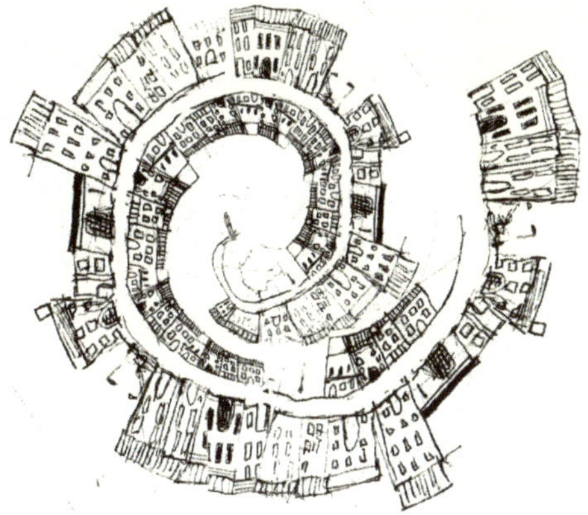

Coiling of Streets

The shift in street direction unwrapped a merry-go-round of street elements: crafted doorways, letterboxes, gates, and window frames with every forward step. The traveller wished to unpeel its facades and flatten them into one image, so they could study the elements in a linear progression.

As the winding pathways brought the opposite building closer, it loomed over the traveller. This slight change in angle created a new focal point every minute or so. New markers appeared—a café named after a painter, an old and powerful family crest on the corner of a building, lights, and signs. Eventually, they would come to know them in sequence, using them to navigate the city. One side was cast in shadow while the other soaked in the sun. The buildings showed their wear, with slightly more paint peeling on the sun-facing facades.

The streets became narrower towards the historic centre. Soon, they began to play tricks on the traveller's perception with their slight curvature. The traveller should have been close to the river by now. What once felt like a straightforward journey was spiralling into a disorienting whirl of shapes and hues. The city coiled around them, streets intertwining in a mesmerising maze.

The traveller quickened their pace, hoping to outpace the dizzying effect of the spiralling streets. Each turn heightened the feeling of being trapped in an endless loop, and anxiety clawed at the edges of their consciousness. They fell into a run, the buildings blurring into streaks of colour, an abstract painting brought to life by their frenzied movements.

The sun, casting longer shadows on one side of the street, now played tricks with the traveller's sense of time. Was the sun setting faster than usual? Was the city conspiring to keep them lost in this perpetual swirl?

Amidst the confusion, a door caught their eye—ajar and inviting. A fixture attached to it gleamed in a sliver of light. It was a brass door knocker of a horse's head that exactly matched one the traveller knew to be located by the ice cream parlour across the city. Without hesitation this time, they entered and exited exactly where they had hoped. A note for future reference: the traveller decided never to take that street route again.

Interlude: The Rhythms of Departure

Arriving early for their departure, the traveller found a seat and took in the surroundings of the bustling train station. The floor, an intentional grid of marble rectangles, directed the flow of people from A to B. However, when suitcases strayed from these paths, a rumble echoed through the station, adding to the symphony of movement. Splinter beams extended to welcome arriving passengers, casting bright light from where the trains emerged, offering a rare glimpse of the outside world through the cloudy windows above. Perhaps this was designed so the traveller wouldn't be distracted by the sky.

Clusters of people continuously formed and dispersed, their belongings seamlessly becoming extensions of their forms. Despite the apparent smoothness, the varying speeds of this orchestrated chaos created a mesmerising mayhem. Filtering out the eruption of various languages, the traveller tried to focus on the tannoy announcements, but the unintelligible sounds left them frustrated. Instead, their attention was drawn to the orange, dotted light board—the key to the journey ahead.

The station was not just a funnel for travellers but for other creatures as well. Sparrows darted through the air, taking sharp corners into adjacent shops. These small birds, mere flickers overhead, landed in cafés to pick up crumbs and nestled into nooks in the stone walls, assessing the area for more. The warm smell of fresh bread wafted through the air, an enticing aroma that explained the attraction of these little brown birds to the station.

Gems Along the Bridge

A necklace adorned with gems was an apt description for the traveller's stroll that day.

As they traversed the busy bridge, they found the foot traffic of fellow travellers even denser than the passing motor vehicles. Amidst the flow, they noticed a charming connection—a pair of lovers on opposite sides of the bridge, their smiles and shared gaze forming an invisible tie between them. The man attempted to capture the perfect moment, positioning his partner confidently against the scenic backdrop of the bridge. Laughter ensued as they both realised the challenge of timing, needing near-perfection to exclude any other passersby from her shot. It was almost heartwarming, the traveller mused, witnessing not frustration but an acceptance of the reality of the chosen spot. The couple, deeply in love, invoked a subtle pang of emotion in the traveller's heart.

This scene contrasted with a memory from the previous week when a woman had asked for their help in capturing her and her partner's moment on a different bridge. Although the traveller willingly took dozens of photos, she remained visually unsatisfied. Later, they observed her seeking the same favour from another stranger, ending with the same disappointment. Her smile only activated in the presence of a lens.

At the opposite end of the bridge, another gem caught their attention. Leaning over the edge, they spotted a snowy egret perched gracefully on the banks, gazing down onto the water. The mirrored perspective created a unique moment, connecting the traveller with the egret as they both observed the surroundings.

They found themself on this bridge for a specific reason: to meet another traveller. Armed with a deeper knowledge of the city, they aimed to facilitate their journey, share stories, and revel in the moment, discovering more gems together.

A Reflection on Identity in Unfamiliar Lands

In the heart of the city, amidst the swirling currents of life, the traveller found themself at a crossroads of identity. The title they had so confidently embraced — "The Curious Observer" — now echoed with an unsettling ambiguity. Their journey, a myriad of woven tales of exploration and discovery, began to unravel at the edges.

From the onset, the traveller had painted themself as the seeker of authenticity, the one who eschewed the well-trodden paths in favour of the hidden gems. They had stood atop metaphorical soapboxes, passionately decrying the "tourist," with their overstuffed itineraries and penchant for crowded attractions. The tourist, in the traveller's narrative, was an intruder, a disruptor of the delicate balance between a place and its people.

Yet, as the traveller revisited the chapters of their own

stories, a disquieting truth began to emerge. The same plazas, the same historical landmarks, the same bustling markets — they had walked the very paths they had deemed too ordinary for a true explorer. The realisation hung heavy in the air, casting a shadow over the once unblemished image of the traveller.

A sense of guilt crept in, accompanied by a nagging question: Were they truly the curious observer, or had they become entangled in the same touristy threads they had criticised? The distinction between the two, once so clear, blurred into a haze of uncertainty.

In search of answers, the traveller embarked on a new quest, not across geographical landscapes but through the corridors of self-reflection. Conversations with fellow wanderers became a mirror, reflecting the shared experiences of seeking, discovering, and yes, occasionally succumbing to the allure of the well-known attractions.

The traveller found comfort in realising that the lines between tourist and traveller were porous, shifting with each step taken in unfamiliar lands. The quest for authenticity, it appeared, was not a black-and-white endeavour but a nuanced exploration of the shades in between.

With this newfound understanding, the traveller assumed the duality of their role. They were both the storyteller and the audience, the curious observer who could find wonder in the ordinary and charm in the touristy. In the end, the journey wasn't about rigid definitions but the fluidity of experiences that painted the canvas of a life well-travelled.

A Poem for an Evening

Hand on the back door of a
dimpled glass doorway,
timber frame and hanging
blue
beads.
Inviting, yet unsettling,

secure
within a
court
yard

Alone outside at night,
A table, two chairs,
feet on cooler evening tiles,
day's warmth slowly dissipating.
Outdoor switch flickers,

fading glow, vivid citron walls.
Matches on table, sliding open the box,
f i n g e r - l e n g t h   m a t c h
strikes,
~~against the red, rough side.~~
Lit now, lemon candles.
Kitchen illuminated,
Odd how clear everything is,
from
the darkness.
Unaware of being the visitor
in another's home.
Reflections by the drain,
a line of light moving,
emerging from the opening.
Thick licorice lace with legs,
countless meandering out,
unaware of the traveller.
Another follows, and another,
trickling off to unknown places,
leaving the traveller wondering.
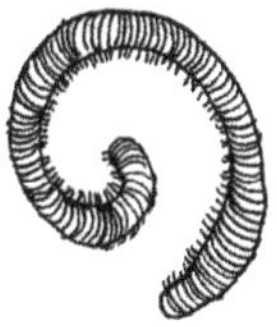
Candle flame flickers its last,
light switched with a click,
door closed with a lock.
Next morning, breakfast in the same space,
new discovery,
one creature curled and motionless on warmed tiles.

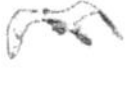

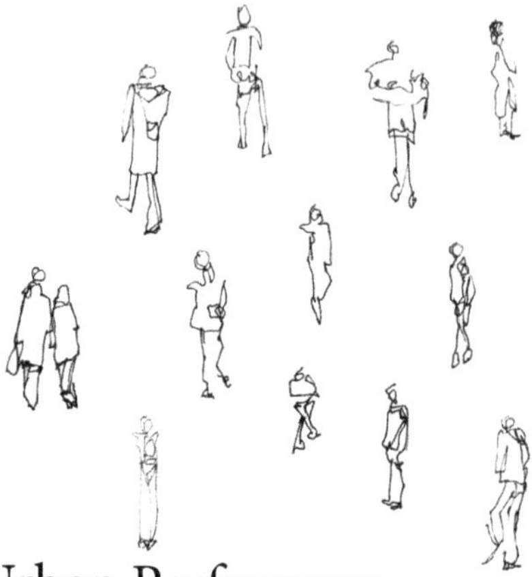

Tales of Urban Performers

In the realm of urban enchantment, street performers took a prominent role, crafting narratives of artistry and survival. Street performers, typically associated with musicians and vocalists, held a unique sway over the perceived atmosphere. Yet, this ensemble extended beyond the expected. Consider the online influencers, staging impromptu performances for the lens, strategically clustered at tourist hubs. In their edits, they erased the surrounding crowd, basking in a spotlight that seemingly belonged solely to them.

Then there was the lady at the cathedral, a daily presence traversing the line, her cup extended, asking for spare change with silent determination. The irony unfolded as the shift towards a cashless society transformed the act into a contactless performance — observers abstained from contributing, engaged in their own subtle acts of resistance.

Among the cautionary figures were the rose vendor, whose offer of a free rose required a fee, and the art peddler, laying traps of printed copies along live paths. However, in between these cautionary tales, a different performer stepped into their narrative.

Late into the evening, a humble man frequented the traveller's favourite café, a familiar face to the bar staff who greeted him with warmth. His espresso was prepared before he even settled into his seat; there was an unspoken camaraderie between this performer and the establishment.

A fortnight later, on stone steps, they witnessed a different kind of performance — a musician serenading a scattered audience. As rain arrived, the crowd dispersed, leaving them contemplating whether to endure the downpour. In this moment of indecision, the café performer reappeared, this time as an umbrella vendor. With the raindrops beginning their descent, they raised their hand to purchase a shield from him.

A few steps away, however, he forgot to hand over the umbrella. The traveller called out after him, laughter ringing in the air. An honest mistake, acknowledged and rectified with an apology and a smile that lingered on their cheeks. In this exchange, they discerned the authenticity of a performer entangled with the way of the city.

Embracing the Winter Shift

In the changing seasons, the allure of witnessing nature's transformation added a layer of beauty to the traveller's experience. When they initially stepped into this place, a warm embrace greeted them at the point before leaves crisped beneath their feet, painting the landscape in hues of autumn brilliance. The once harsh sun cast a softer glow, gently illuminating the world as if it had exchanged its earlier intensity for a more subtle radiance, saturating the colours with the morning dew.

The temperature shift was pronounced, keenly observed through the city's inhabitants, who responded with long winter coats, hats, and scarves. Even their four-legged companions were outfitted in cosy coats, much to the traveller's amusement. The brisk air imparted a quickened pace to the city's beat. Beyond the urban core, local areas seemed to hush slightly, with more people opting for indoor sanctuaries to escape the cooling outdoors. Although crowds remained, the atmosphere changed; people lingered less, and there was a different sound, a more subdued hum that reflected the transition into winter.

Yet, amidst the changing scenery, in the streets that drew to the heart of the city pulsed with life. The streets became a festive scene illuminated by thousands of stars. Music wove through the air as more musicians graced the squares and narrow paving playing their wooden instruments. The distant melody invited a respectful parting in the clusters of people, as if an invisible stage had been set, and the sound required a space to breathe. The luminous strings of lights connected buildings, creating a canopy that sheltered passersby below as they engaged in the delightful activity of window shopping, peering into beautifully curated displays of craftsmanship, culture, and organisation. The city, in its winter garb, became a tapestry of lights, music, and shared moments, inviting the traveller to immerse themselves in the enchanting taste of seasonal change.

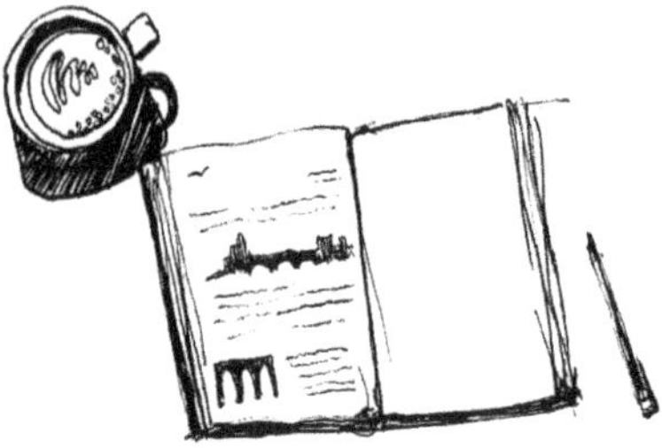

Trilogy of Arches

On the day when the air offered warmth with gentle kisses of wind, the traveller's pace slowed, allowing them a more leisurely browse of the cityscape. As the traveller roamed the city's streets, a recurring motif of three arches presented itself in multiple moments in their meander. Whether supporting a bridge's weight or adorning the entrance to a grand building, the architectural triads seemed to follow them around all corners.

Beneath the bridge, three sturdy arches held the structure aloft, its reflection skittering shards on the moving current below. And atop these bridges, another three arches framed vistas of distant hillsides and the central river. Even the facades of ancient buildings bore the mark of three arches.

In the city's museums and galleries, triptychs of paintings depicted scenes steeped in history, each panel framed by three arches. And in the neighbouring city's ruins of baths, the same trio of arches adorned the entrance to idyllic country scenes, hinting at a shared heritage.

The traveller now found themself sitting in their café, pondering. Lost in thought while sketching, they looked down to see these arches subconsciously etched in their journal as they stared out of the window. Even this café was composed of three expansive glass arches. It was then that they resolved to uncover the meaning behind this recurring symbol.

Their quaint quest began with the coffee barista, who suggested that the triad of arches symbolise structural strength and stability like that found at the bridge. There were two other reasons that the barista couldn't remember off the top of their head. They turned to a colleague in question but they too were unable to provide the other answers. The traveller, unsatisfied with this singular explanation, pressed on, determined to collect the other truths.

Next, they thought best to head to the markets, where conversations were a pot of bubbles and babbles. It wasn't long before one merchant directed the traveller to another, bellowing over the business of buyers. The merchant they encountered was peddling trinkets of colour and jewels. Upon an agreement of one for coin and answer, the merchant spoke of the arches representing past, present, and future—a cycle of time captured in stone. Thankful, the traveller departed from the busy square. Still, the traveller sought the elusive third answer.

Their afternoon was filled with conversations, yet none yielded the final answer. The traveller's inquiries had ignited a thirst for knowledge among the populace, fostering a growing reliance on others to possess the elusive third answer. An insatiable desire to uncover the truth spread through the city like wildfire. It appeared that the significance of the third arch had been relegated to the annals of forgotten lore. The traveller pondered when it was last spoken of and by whom.

As evening descended and the city's streets surrendered to darkness, the traveller meandered through dimly lit alleys, their mind consumed by thoughts of the arches. The chill caught up to them, and the lights of a corner pub offered heat they required. After picking a drink from the bar they found a quiet corner, having no luck with the barmaid on the third arch, they had been asking around too.

A few sips into their sharp drink a figure slid into a seat opposite theirs. Hunched over in a dark jacket and tattered scarf, an old man leaned over the table to speak to the traveller over the noise of the pub, "I know the answer you seek."

"You do?" the traveller said eagerly, "I've been thinking all day and night about it, it's an itch in my mind that I cannot scratch."

"Why do you think I should share it with you? It has been long forgotten, no one cared for it so why should it begin again?" The man scratched his beard, seemingly testing the traveller.

"Tell me why you are so reluctant to share this tale with me?"

The man grunted his reply, "I know the answer you seek," his annoyance evident in the tone of his voice. "I've been hearing the questions, leading back to you. Your mention of the third has brought it back to life, your inquiry now boiling over. Do you truly wish to know?"

The traveller saw the shake of irritation that festered within him, he explained, "this feeling born of years spent watching society disregard the wisdom of the past. Why should I share this forgotten tale with someone who only seeks it out of idle curiosity? Why should I breathe life back into a story that the world had long ago cast aside? Why do you think I should share it with you?" he continued to challenge, his frustration bubbling to the surface. "It has been long forgotten, ignored by all. Why should it matter now?"

As he spoke, the traveller saw a surge of resentment towards the nature of modern life, towards those who sought knowledge only for personal gain or fleeting entertainment. What right did they have to intrude upon the sanctity of tradition, to demand answers to questions they had no right to ask?

For a minute the traveller thought in silence, contemplating what the man had shared. They met eyes with the man and said, "I understand the weight of your hesitation, but consider this: stories, like the one you hold within you, are the threads that bind us to our past, our present, and our future. They are the echoes of our shared humanity, the vessels through which our collective experiences are preserved and passed down through generations. Without storytellers, without keepers of memories like yourself, these threads would fray and fade into oblivion, lost to time. By sharing the answer you hold, you breathe new life into this forgotten tale, ensuring that it continues to resonate in the hearts and minds of those who hear it. In doing so, you become a steward of our shared history, a guardian of our cultural heritage. So, I implore you, not for my sake alone, but for the sake of all who come after us, share with me the wisdom of the third arch, and let its story be heard once more. But if you share the story with me, I promise to carry it forward, to share it back with everyone I've spoken to today. Together, we can ensure that this story lives on, that it's not forgotten."

The old man grunted sceptically, "Hmph... Fine. Tell me, traveller, do you swear by this promise?"

The traveller nodded solemnly. "I swear by it, with all my heart."

"Very well then," the old man relented. "Listen closely, and I shall tell you the tale of the third arch."

As the old man began to speak, his words carried the weight of centuries past. “Long ago, in the time of our ancestors,” he began, “the city was a fortress, a bastion against the tides of time and turmoil. The three arches were more than just marvels; they were symbols of our resilience, our strength in the face of adversity.”

He described how each arch stood together, guarding the city against invaders and providing a gateway to safety for those within. “In those days, the city was a beacon of hope,” he continued. “The three arches were our bastions of strength, our protectors in times of need. They symbolised not just physical strength, but the unity and resilience of our community, standing as guardians of our shared history and culture.”

As the traveller listened, they couldn’t help but feel a sense of awe at the depth of history. Each stone, each arch, held a story waiting to be told, following from the resilience of those who came before.

As the old man’s tale drew to a close, the traveller felt an overwhelming sense of gratitude for the wisdom shared. With a newfound understanding of the city’s history, the traveller journeyed homeward, their steps lighter, their heart fuller. In the gentle glow of streetlights, the arches stood as guardians of a legacy that would endure long after they were gone. And in that moment, the traveller knew that they had become a part of something greater—a story woven into the very fabric of the cityscape.

An Encounter with a Dragon

In the labyrinthine bustle of the city, whispers of dragons sang their way into the traveller's ears – mythical beings carved in stone, perched atop gates, and adorning flickering lanterns. Little did the traveller anticipate encountering a living, breathing dragon within the confines of a quaint antique store.

Drawn by the tales of dragons and the glint of treasures, the traveller found themself by chance at the entrance of an unassuming store. An aged display window, offering just a glimpse of the trove within, piqued the traveller's curiosity. The slumbering lady, settled in a wide tanned leather armchair inside, seemed an integral part of the shop. Her presence seemed reminiscent of a bird nestled in its meticulously crafted nest, embodying a sense of comfort and contentment within the curated haven she had clearly spent years building. The traveller, wary not to disturb her peaceful repose, briefly peered through the window. It almost felt like an intrusion into her private abode, given how comfortably she tucked into the expansive armchair. The late hour suggested that the store was possibly her dwelling too, open to those who chanced upon it in the quiet evening.

The desire to uncover hidden gems became irresistible, and so, the traveller moved to linger at the entrance, peering through the doorway, wedged open by a well-worn wooden block, an antique itself. Warm, musty notes found their way into the traveller's nostrils; stagnant age. There was nothing from the traveller's years that they'd find in this curio emporium.

The brief step into the doorway and the store was a web of history. The shop appeared unable to contain the dimensions of the surrounding streets, creating an illusion of overflow. Everything within the store, from the aged paintings stacked against cluttered walls to the tarnished brass and shiny objects that caught the traveller's eye, was arranged with a precision that belied the limited space. The traveller felt it cluttered but found the word insulting to each individual treasure that sat among one another.

The desire to sift through each item grew stronger – a yearning to unearth a rare treasure buried within the mass of antiques. The air, thick with the scent of time, and the ambiance suggested that every item had a story waiting to be uncovered.

But the traveller's eyes reverted back to the old woman sunken in her seat; something seemed amiss. It wasn't the woman that the curious observer needed to be observing but the seat that she sat in. Its claw-footed elements appeared relaxed to the floor, talons outstretched on the tiles, not the typical expected design. The back of the chair inflated and deflated against the woman. The traveller couldn't see where the chair stopped; following one side, the chair snaked into a curl many feet away, it could've been a small mat. The other side disappeared behind stacks of objects, but the skin was still noticeable amongst the brass stacks around the corner of the shop. Its end was found resting half a dozen shelves up in the form of a dragon's sleeping head. A gold amber orb, like the streetlights of the city, unfolded as this creature awoke, eye set on the traveller before drifting lazily back into sleep. The traveller almost thought they had imagined it.

Captivated and cautious, the traveller refrained from stepping inside, leaving the dragon undisturbed in its slumber, swiftly turning on their heels and heading back into the streetlight night of dark that would forever remind them of the night they encountered a dragon.

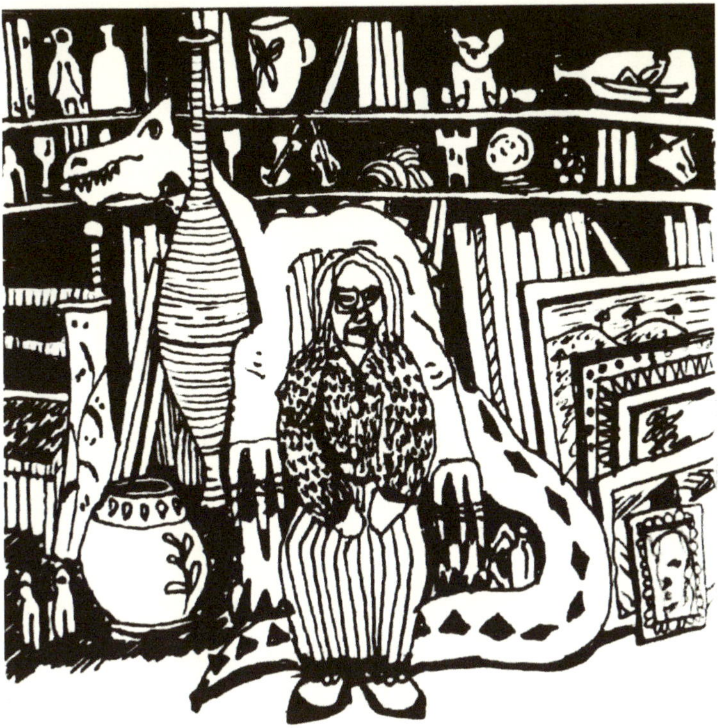

Treasures in Teaspoons

Meandering through a midnight market, where wares of all kinds enticed wanderers, the traveller wrapped their coat tightly around themselves in the coming winter's air and darkening sky. Excitement bubbled with each enchanting stall, each one selling different items from the last.

The traveller was there for an item, something to symbolise and encapsulate their journey as it neared its end. This thought slightly puzzled the traveller. They thought the concept of "having" and "owning" warranted deeper examination, particularly in the context of human perception and attachment to material possessions.

"To have" meant something was in one's physical or mental grasp at a given moment. When one spoke of "having" something in the present tense, there was often an implicit assumption of permanence, an unwavering sense of possession and eternal ownership. However, reality dictated that all things were transient. The juxtaposition prompted the question: did possession culminate in the object's demise or the owner's departure? Despite the inevitability of endings, there was a persistent belief in the enduring nature of possessions, often tethered to us in perpetuity. Yet the illusion of permanence was proven false by time, as exemplified by the decay of once-cherished artefacts or the fading of cherished memories.

Perception of ownership was rooted in a desire for permanence, but the reality was that all things were fleeting. However, this inclination towards permanence was not inherently negative; it spoke to the innate desire for stability and continuity in a world characterised by constant change. These possessions often served as anchors, grounding us in familiar terrain amidst these eroding coastlines.

The concept of "having" extended beyond possession; it was an active engagement with the world, a continuous process of acquisition and relinquishment. To "have" was to participate in life, to embrace the human experience.

Consider the essence of this encapsulated in the phrase "to have until." To have dreams, the whispered tales in the night, told stories of memory until the stir of dawn's awakening gently nudged them from slumber, leaving naught but a trace lingering just out of reach

To have friendship with shared laughter and whispered secrets remained steadfast until the tug of fate fractured the entwined, leading each soul down its own winding road. To have youth, the sprites of age danced with abandon, until time's hands began to spin the silver strands into memory, a reflection back to youth from the vantage point of age. To have a love, an intertwining of souls so intense that each was imprinted upon the other, and when severed, left in agony, crying out into the emptiness for a call that would never be returned. These examples underscored the impermanence inherent in the act of "having," a reminder that each carried within it the seeds of its own ending.

The concept of "having" was multifaceted, fraught with implications for human perception and experience. It was a reflection of our transient existence, a reminder of the impermanence that defined our journey through life. It was to cherish, to hold with reverence the fleeting moments of existence. Indeed, to "have" was to acknowledge the finite nature of life.

And so when the traveller discovered a drawer stacked full of exquisite cutlery with delicately crafted spoons, forks, and knives gleaming with a quiet elegance, their fingers grazed upon a golden teaspoon adorned with a detailed design—a mythical creature delicately etched into the handle. It was the find that they were after; it resonated with the spirit of the city they wandered through every day.

Intrigued by this golden spoon, the traveller acquired it. A lady adorned in bangles, sounding like their sift through the cutlery drawer, wrapped up the item for the traveller to pocket.

As the exchange concluded with a bid adieu, the traveller felt a sense of anticipation, knowing that they had acquired more than just a piece of cutlery—they had obtained a cherished artefact, envisioning it as a token reminder of their solo exploration.

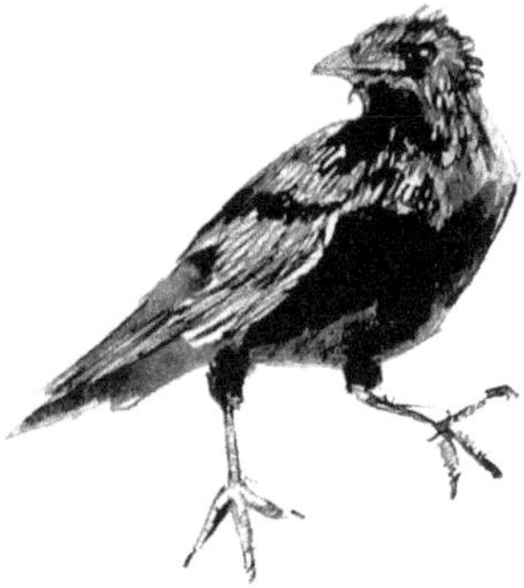

The Crow's Call

Taptaptap. Taptaptap. Taptaptap.

In the quiet predawn hours the traveller awoke with a jolt. They discovered the persistent sound was not a figment of their imagination but an insistent tapping outside their window. Peeling off their thin sheets with confusion and panic they moved off their bed and toward the source of the noise.

Rolling up the blinds, they were met with the silhouette of a crow, tapping impatiently on the window frame. *Taptaptap.*

Unlocking the window, they opened it only at a degree, which was enough for a beak to poke through.

"What do you want? What time is it?" the traveller grumbled, peering at the dark blue sky beyond, no sign of the sun.

“You owe me a favour. I need it today,” its eyes fixed on the traveller

“Fine but you could’ve come at noon, I like my mornings to myself.” The traveller retorted with a scowl, hoping the crow would feel some guilt for waking them at this ungodly hour.

“I’ll come back at noon. Be ready.”

“For what?” But as the words fell from their lips the crow had hopped and taken flight, leaving the traveller with a creeping morning chill that drew them back to the warmth of their bed. They had better remember to wake back up.

The traveller sat in the shade of the pigeon park sheltered by burnt amber leaves. Benches were sparse and the traveller seemed to be the only person there. The crow arrived soon after their arrival, swooping down from a nearby branch and landing at the traveller’s side.

“I need you to retrieve an item for me. It has been stolen from my nest by another” the crow hopped onto the arm rest to meet the traveller’s gaze. “A magpie, none too wise, stole it when I wasn’t aware. The item glows with an amber heart.”

“Why do you need me? What can I do?” questioned the traveller, their eyes searching for understanding.

“You owe a favour. As you are soon to leave this city,

your debt must be paid. I am unable to enter where the creature dwells. I believe you are a mediator between the mundane and the magical. You possess a special affinity that can bridge the gap between realms."

The traveller's eyes narrowed with a mix of curiosity and reluctance. "What assurance do I have that this favour will truly settle my debt? And why do I get the sense that retrieving this 'glowing amber heart' won't be a walk in the park?" The traveller made a gesture at their current location.

The crow cawed softly, its beady eyes reflecting a sense of understanding. "You doubt the nature of debts and favours, traveller. But rest assured, once you aid me in this, our transaction will be complete. As for the challenge that lies ahead, remember that challenges are the essence of adventures. Embrace the unknown, and you may find more than you seek."

The traveller sighed, a mixture of resignation and acceptance crossing their features. "Alright, crow. I'll do it. But after this, no more unexpected visits, and no more debts, understood?"

The traveller and crow stood outside the iron gates, the only entrance they could see in the walled garden. Gathering that the crow could go no further, the traveller entered through a wider gap at the edge of the gate.

It was old and broken, swinging on remaining hinges. People walked past, but no one eyed them, as if they were entering a realm unseen. Inside, four columns stood on corners of a square, each a podium for curly haired babes cast in a terracotta. On the edge of the gate a stone eagle watched the overgrown garden. Vines grew over statues covered in algae. There was no caretaker, no gardener to preen. It was odd, the other gardens the traveller visited always appeared prim and proper.

Their footsteps moved forward on loose stones. Surveying the debris and overgrown elements. The garden was quiet, no person in sight. The path lapped around the perimeter with smaller foliage in the middle and trees lining the outside path.

A few laps around the site and the traveller wasn't sure what to do. They removed their coat and placed it as a blanket on the ground, and so they waited. And waited. And waited.

The traveller could feel the presence of sunset as cold kissed the air just as a line of movement caught the traveller's attention. From the distant conifer tree, a magpie took flight. The traveller hoped it was the particular magpie. They waited a moment to approach the tree. At its base the traveller looked up to spot a nest up at quite the height.

A secondary wall of crumbling bricks left a stairwell of sorts beside the tree. The traveller examined the remnants of bricks creating a precarious ascent. After a moment's hesitation, they decided to climb, their fingers testing the stability of each brick.

Reaching the top of the makeshift stairwell, the traveller found themself at eye level with the magpie's abandoned nest. It was a chaotic arrangement of twigs, feathers, and assorted trinkets.

Knowing that the magpie had taken flight and left the nest, the traveller carefully peered over. They spotted a glimmering object nestled among the twigs, catching the last rays of sunlight.

As the traveller reached for the item, a sudden rustle of wings overhead made them look up. The magpie, perched on a higher branch, observed the scene. It seemed the bird had returned, perhaps hesitant to completely abandon its treasure.

The interruption caused the traveller unease in their balance at the height they clung. A slight slip of footing, the traveller kicked a brick from underneath splitting from the wall, as did the one under. The chain of chaos unfolded, the wall was crumbling and the traveller was tumbling.

A series of sharp movements without thought, only instinct driving the traveller. They scaled down, leaving the nest behind. Falling debris followed the traveller with Each point of descent. But towards the last few steps, the pressure forced another slip and they fell face down onto the stone path. Knees and palms taking the landing. The traveller groaned and grunted, cursing the crow and the singeing sensation from the fall.

One magpie was indeed for sorrow, the traveller thought.

Picking themself onto two feet, they could now study what the crow had stolen from them.

The drop-shaped gem with a golden glow, casting a luminous aura that hummed with an inner fire. Its clarity was impeccable. Whispers of ancient secrets seemed to linger within the incredulous amount of facets and depth.

The traveller pocketed the crow's treasure. They exited the garden to follow the streets home through the broken down wall. Passers by took notice of the hole and of the garden, pausing in intrigue. Maybe the traveller had accidentally opened a door into a forgotten space. Before they made their turn down another street they looked back to find a few wanderers floating into the overgrown garden, maybe someone would tend to it now.

As they contemplated the jewel, near enough at their abode, they looked up to the fluttering movement overhead.

Seven magpies in flight.

Seven for a secret never to be told.

A Recovery of the Lost

Lost in the city of nooks and crannies, the traveller's desperation to recover their misplaced possession grew with each fruitless inquiry. It wasn't until the dusk settled, casting long shadows on the cobblestone streets, that a familiar silhouette emerged—the man who had once saved the traveller from an ill-fated plunge into mysterious puddles.

With a knowing smile, the mysterious man approached the distressed traveller. "Troubled seeker, I sense the weight of your search. Have you truly checked everywhere?" he inquired, his eyes holding a glint of ancient understanding.

The traveller, wearied by their quest, nodded in reluctant admission. "Every nook, every cranny, every corner I could think of. It's as if the city has swallowed my belonging whole," the traveller confessed.

The mysterious man's gaze lingered for a moment before he spoke, "Ah, but have you truly explored all realms? Sometimes, the answers lie beyond the scope of eyes but within the grasp of the mind."

As he uttered those words, the man handed the traveller a small slip of parchment, then faded into the evening shadows as swiftly as he had appeared.

Perplexed, the traveller found warmth in a nearby café. Stirring their cup absentmindedly, the rhythmic clink of the spoon against porcelain echoed like distant water droplets. The riddle unfolded before them on the piece of paper, a puzzle of cryptic verse that teetered on the edge of comprehension.

I'm a ribbon unseen, yet I shape the land,
Invisible threads, a puzzle unplanned.
From heights unknown, I chart my course,
A lifeline of cities, a hidden force.
Silent whispers in the air I send,
Bridging gaps, my journey has no end.
Carving valleys, guiding each source,
A clandestine architect, a secret discourse.

As the traveller pondered each line, the stirring motion mirrored the gentle flow of a river. Suddenly, a realisation dawned—an epiphany akin to the uncovering of hidden currents. The river.

Leaving the café in renewed determination, the traveller followed the course of their realisation. Along the winding streets, past squares, until they reached one of the city's edges. There, under the moonlit sky, the river murmured its secrets.

And there, nestled against the riverbank, was the lost possession. The traveller, perplexed, realised they had not ventured to this side of the riverbank before; they had merely observed from a distance. How, then, had their possession found its way to this hidden alcove?

Approaching the bank where grass met water, the traveller extended their hand to retrieve the lost item, fingers grazing the cool surface. A misstep on the moistened grass sent them tumbling, but instead of plunging into the river, they emerged unscathed, the mysterious man having pulled them back from the brink.

"Are you following me?" the traveller's face contorted with a mix of anger and suspicion. "Did you take my possession and hide it here, intending for me to fall into the river?"

The shadow-man tilted his head curiously, a gesture reminiscent of another enigmatic figure the traveller had encountered—the crow. "I only meant to help, for your travels soon conclude, and homeward you must be. Many things you have seen, but remain here you do not want to be," he spoke in riddles, his form dissipating into the encroaching shadows, leaving the traveller pondering.

As the shadows enveloped the mysterious man, the traveller sensed a subtle shift in the air, akin to tuning into a different frequency on a radio. With a lingering gaze, they turned their back to the riverbanks and started the journey homeward. Yet, amidst the familiar sounds of the surroundings, they couldn't shake the feeling of echoes calling from behind the trickling water—a mysterious resonance from another dimension, reverberating through time and realms.

The lost possession now safely cradled, the traveller couldn't shake the feeling that their encounters with these mysterious beings were integral components in a larger composition, intricately connected to the narrative unfolding in the traveller's journey.

Reflections on Familiarity in the Cityscape

As the traveller meandered through the familiar streets of the city they now called home, a contemplative air enveloped their thoughts. Once perturbed by the leisurely pace of newcomers, laden with cumbersome luggage that obstructed the thoroughfares, the traveller then viewed such scenes through a lens of fond nostalgia. These encounters, once a source of mild irritation, had transformed into cherished symbols of the city's essence.

Amidst the course of the city, the traveller paused to reflect on the nature of first encounters. They acknowledged the irreplaceable allure of that inaugural arrival, a moment bubbling with anticipation and novelty that could never be replicated. Each subsequent engagement with the cityscape was coloured by the imprint of past experiences, imbuing each visitation with a distinct flavour of reminiscence.

Observing the wide-eyed wonder of newcomers as they marvelled at the city's architectural splendours and cultural landmarks, the traveller was reminded of their own initial foray into this urban landscape. A pang of longing stirred within them, a yearning to rekindle the fervour of discovery that had once ignited their soul. Yet, tempered by the depth of understanding and intimacy cultivated over time, they found relief in the familiarity of their surroundings.

While the traveller navigated the city with practised ease, their footsteps guided by an intimate knowledge of its complex streets, there remained an indelible hunger to reclaim the mantle of the initiate. They longed to immerse themself once more in the heady rush of first-time exploration, to rediscover the city's hidden gems with fresh eyes and unbridled enthusiasm. And so, in the throng of suitcases and astir crowds, the traveller found themself wanting for a return to that ephemeral state of newness, where every corner held the promise of discovery and adventure.

A Parting of Paths

As the traveller made their way to the river, the evening air enveloped them in serenity. Leaning against one of the ancient stone walls, they paused to take in the scene before them. It was their final night in this city, and instead of watching the sunset from the familiar hilltop, they had chosen to soothe their soul by the riverside, where the water shimmered with the last rays of daylight.

With each breath, the atmosphere was infused with the crisp scent of the nearby river and the earthy aroma of grass. The city began to stir as restaurants opened their doors, and the homely smells of freshly prepared meals wafted through the air.

Through the three graceful arches of the bridge, the traveller's gaze drifted to the river below, where a lone rower glided effortlessly under. The rhythmic motion of the oars caught the traveller's attention as they contemplated this story's end.

Despite the solitude of their last evening in the city, the traveller found comfort in the energy surrounding them. Alone, yet not lonely, they lived the moment, allowing themself to be swept up in the cityscape.

The flap of wings shifted their attention, sending a chill of the wind to kiss the traveller's cheek. The crow alighted nearby to where the traveller leaned against the stone wall. Its dark form silhouetted against the fading light. Without a word of greeting, the traveller reached into their pocket and retrieved a stone, cool in their palm and twiddled it thoughtfully between their fingers.

"This is quite an important possession to you," they remarked, their voice calm and measured. The crow hesitated, taking a few tentative steps forward before retreating one, its beak tilted downward in contemplation.

Leaning against the weathered stone wall, the traveller turned to the crow, the diamond glinting in their hand. "Tell me crow, where did you acquire this precious stone, and why?" they asked, their voice calm yet tinged with curiosity.

The crow hesitated for a moment, its beady eyes darting back and forth. "It matters not where I found it or why," it croaked cryptically. "What matters is that it has found its way to you."

"Tell me or I won't return it," the traveller played.

The crow fixed its sharp gaze on the traveller, its piercing eyes unblinking. "I took it from a dead man on a battlefield," they replied bluntly. "Found it whilst feasting on his eyes, saw it poking out of his pocket. A couple of centuries back if I remember correctly."

Shuddering, the traveller extended their hand, offering the diamond back quickly to its rightful owner. But the crow did not meet their hand. So, they gave the stone a light toss towards the crow, expecting it to deftly catch it in its beak.

However, much to their surprise, the crow's reaction was less than graceful. With a squawk of alarm, it flapped its wings wildly, narrowly avoiding the incoming gemstone. The diamond whacked off the crow's beak, a near miss, and with a plop, disappeared into the murky depths of the river below.

For a moment, there was stunned silence, broken only by the gentle lapping of the river against the shore. The traveller and the crow turned to each other in slight silent horror, both realising what had just transpired.

"Well, that's one way to make a splash," the crow quipped, its voice tinged with amusement.

With a shake of its feathers, the crow regarded the traveller with a wry grin. "Well, it seems the river has claimed it now," it remarked. "But fear not, for some treasures are meant to be lost, while others are waiting to be found."

"Until our paths cross again, wanderer," and with that,

the crow spread its wings and took flight, disappearing into the gathering dusk. Left alone by the riverbank, the traveller couldn't help but chuckle at the absurdity of it all, wondering what new adventures awaited them on their journey ahead.

Echoes of City and Kin

The traveller arrived at the station with more than luggage weighing them down. The gravity of the impending journey was pressing upon them. Releasing their bags on the floor, they stole a moment of respite, cherishing the stillness before the storm of departure. The train, tardy in its arrival, bestowed an unexpected pause for contemplation. Leaning back on a railing, reflections about this journey cascaded through their mind. There was no exhalation of relief; instead, a solemn acknowledgment pervaded—an amalgamation of the sorrowful parting from the city and the yearning for the comforting embrace of loved ones. It was not the terminus; rather, it signified a poignant commencement—a return to the familiar with a heart heavy with memories.

Now, standing on the platform, they realised they were

not ready to embark on the return trip, the inception of this voyage eluded definition. Was it the physical departure or the birth of the idea itself that initiated this emotional odyssey? Regardless, the traveller found themself at the crossroads, having bid adieu to their transient abode. The train tracks stretched before them, heralding the onset of the journey homeward. It wasn't fair, they wished for more time.

In this instance, a memory thought to be far tucked away surfaced at speed, reminiscent of farewells to a parent in younger years. Those sporadic meetings left them perplexed, questioning the intervals between encounters. Yet, the moments spent together held a timeless quality, as if the universe conspired to erase the temporal gaps. During these leave-takings, the traveller both acknowledged the longing for more frequent reunions, grappling with the bittersweet awareness that the sporadic visits were insufficient to fill the void. The poignant symmetry between leaving the city and bidding farewell to a loved one deepened, an emotional resonance underscoring the interconnectedness of places and people in their heart.

The ache that enveloped them now mirrored the one etched in their parent's eyes. Stepping onto the train platform, a forced stillness pervaded—the stiffness of suppressing emotions that threatened to manifest as physical pain. They recognised the need for release but stole themself, a quiet strength in the face of overwhelming emotions. The child within noticed the same in their parent, an unspoken bond of shared sorrow. A welling of tears became a silent acknowledgment of the shared pain. The desire to linger, to explore further, intensified; this time was never enough. Yet, with a heavy heart, they ascended the train steps, signalling the finality of the homeward journey.

The station, shrouded in the late morning quietude, mirrored the hushed sorrow within them. The memory of leaving their parent resurfaced, the echo of shared pain reverberating through the years. They whispered the mantra, not sure whether out loud or in the mind. Words that were a balm to soothe a present discomfort. Though deep down, they knew it was a promise they could never fully keep, that would crack over time like roots through the toughest of stone. They reassured themself, as they always had, that this ache would pass.

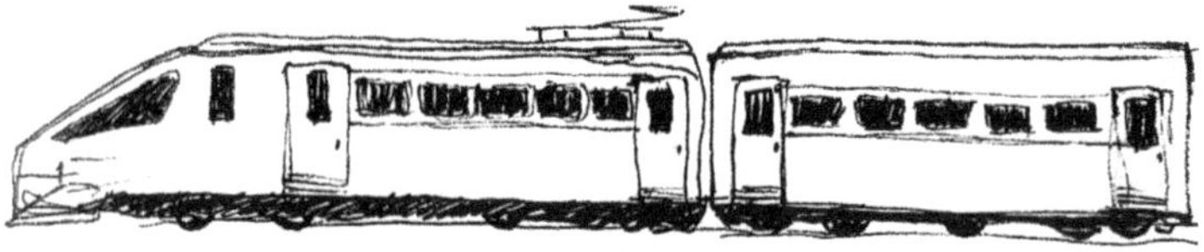

A Prelude to Your Next Chapter Fellow Traveller

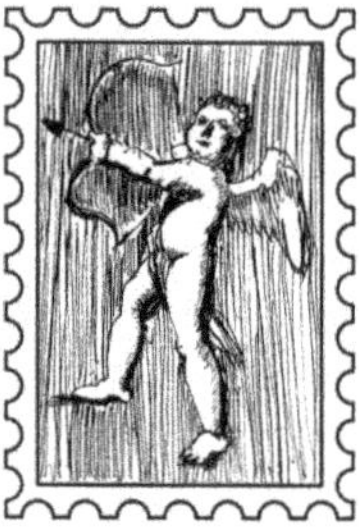

Acknowledgements

Firstly, I must acknowledge myself for taking that brave step as a curious observer and venturing beyond the boundaries I had unknowingly confined myself to. Embracing the world of possibilities made all the difference. Giving myself the time and space to live, breathe, and pursue my passions has been instrumental in shaping this book and my personal growth.

Thank you to my mum, whose virtual companionship over countless cups of tea and the occasional glass of wine during my time in Florence provided warmth and solace amidst the distance.

Thank you to Irene, whose support and infectious enthusiasm lifted my spirits and kept me excited about this book's prospects. Whenever I felt down, your positivity and encouragement cheered me up and renewed my passion for this project. Your excitement was truly contagious, and for that, I am deeply grateful.

Thank you to my muse, my companion, and my best friend. Though our paths have diverged, the inspiration and support you provided were vital to the completion of this book. We were two currents in different flowing rivers, but just as rivers find each other at sea, I hold onto the hope that our paths will cross again someday. Your presence in my life inspired many chapters of this work, and the memories of our time at Viareggio will always hold a special place in my heart. You always believed in me, and for that, you will always have my heart.

I extend my heartfelt thanks to my cherished friends and family for their unyielding encouragement, sending waves of love to every narrative I crafted.

A special acknowledgment to the fellow wanderers I encountered on this journey, sharing stories so full of soul. La Cite, a haven of inspiration, deserves my sincere appreciation. From dawn till dusk, its welcoming tone provided the backdrop for countless hours of creativity. The eclectic playlists of great taste will be missed.

To Emma, laughter was our language, and our hours in La Cite, concocting vampirical mysteries, sipping limoncello and aperitifs, remain treasured memories.

The team at ACES, thank you for your encouragement and support!

To all those who have crossed my path, whether as mentors, friends, or sources of inspiration, thank you for your unwavering support and encouragement. Your belief in me has fuelled my determination to explore new horizons, to love and nurture myself along the way.

Finally, I extend my deepest appreciation to the readers who embark on this journey with me. Your curiosity and open-mindedness are the driving forces behind this book, and I am eternally grateful for your presence.

With heartfelt thanks,

Kenzie

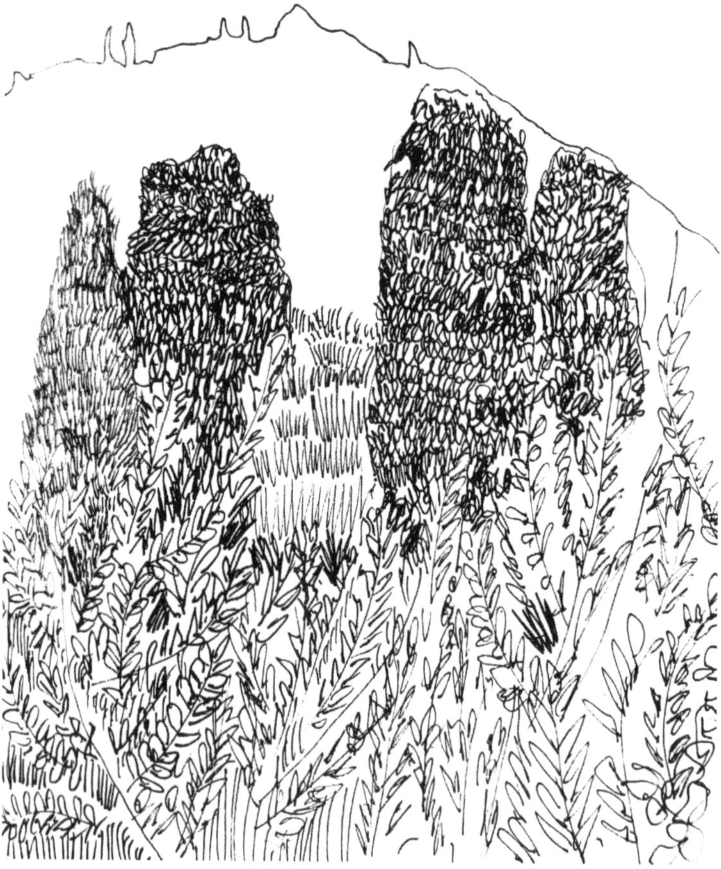

Milton Keynes UK
Ingram Content Group UK Ltd.
UKHW030746100924
448141UK00004B/198

9 781068 715945